PRAY FOR ONE

AND 41 DAY PRAYER & DEVOTION GUIDE

Bo Chancey

Pray for One and 41 Day Prayer & Devotion Guide
Published by 41Press

For information or bulk sales:

41PRESS
Attn: Publishing Team
7200 Queens Place
Amarillo, TX 79109

publisher@41press.com

ISBN: 978-0-578-13053-8

Contents

GIVE ME ONE

chapter one

GIVE ME ONE

I begin with confession.

Confession generally makes everyone uncomfortable, so it is probably not the most strategic way to start a book. I guess that I am okay with this being a bit on the weird side. If you are like me, you have most likely tried normal and found it to be lacking in the satisfaction department.

So let us throw convention to the side and allow the awkwardness to ensue.

I confess that I believe in what Praying for One is all about to an extreme level. I am living out the methodology side of Praying for One. It is ingrained in my DNA. I am immersed in the results. I am a passionate believer in the transformational power of this simple prayer.

I confess that my zeal provides an edge to my words that may cut deeper than intended. I have no desire to wound needlessly, and I have no axe to grind, but my personal failures in following Jesus drive me to share the blessed hope of fruitful living with ever-increasing fervor.

I confess that I have wasted much of my life in vain attempts to make Christianity into something it cannot be. I have stumbled and bumbled through one self-generated mess after another. I have jumped on spiritual bandwagons, followed the hottest trends, and allowed Jesus to become little more than a pop-culture icon in my life. I tried to make Christianity about me instead of about Jesus. My primary motivation was for Jesus to serve me and make my life better instead of me serving Him to expand His Kingdom.

I confess that I have dabbled in many forms of legalism. Okay...that is not true. I have not just dabbled; I have been a full-on legalism addict. I have turned from grace to all kinds of rules and regulations. I know the foolishness of it, but my desire to compete and be better than other Christians was insatiable. I have slandered and demeaned other servants of Jesus because I felt inferior to them and I was jealous of their success.

I confess to feeling great frustration regarding my failures. I am saddened by the ways I have degraded the gospel of Jesus. I grieve over lost time and actions that were detrimental to others. I cannot stand the thought that others might have been following me when I was not in step with Christ. What manner of false doctrine might I have imparted to them?

I confess my tendency to project my flaws onto others. Any perceived finger pointing found within this book will include me at the front of the line. My intent is not to chastise but to encourage and inspire. I have found something great, and I want everyone to experience it.

I confess that I am afraid of what you will think of me. I want you to like me. I want you to like my book. I want you to think things like, "Wow, that Bo Chancey is one sharp cookie!" I don't even know what that means, but I want you to think it.

I confess the truth. I have found purpose beyond self. I have found meaning beyond mere religious expressions. I have found a practical way to connect to God, to others, and to the mission of Jesus.

Praying for One is awesome. I am in awe of how something so simple provides a path for deep growth and eternal fruit. The accessibility of this call to action removes discipleship barriers. Anyone can pray for One. There are no prerequisites. This prayer is a wonderful next step for anyone desiring to live the life for which we were all created.

Pray for One is not an evangelistic program or a trendy church-growth strategy. Pray for One is about becoming like Jesus and thus doing what He would do. Pray for One is discipleship in three words.

What was Jesus like? What motivated Him?

We see His heart very clearly when Jesus taught about a shepherd and his sheep. You see, Jesus is consumed with the One. What does He say? If a shepherd has 100 sheep and One of them wanders away, he will leave the 99 to look for the One. Jesus is that kind of shepherd, and He is passionately fixated on finding the One. If we are true followers of Jesus, then we too must become passionately consumed with His mission of finding the One.

The premise is simple, and it is imperative that we refrain from complicating it.

Just ask God to give you One person to share His love with. Pray that He would place someone, anyone, in your path to share the gospel with. As often as you pray, pray for One. Allow your primary prayers to move beyond prayers for self into prayers for One. Seek first His Kingdom and His righteousness. Instead of just praying for promotions, protection, and provision, plead first for One.

Bombard the throne with passionate prayers for One. Drive your God crazy with the zealous request for One. Approach the throne of grace with extreme confidence that you are requesting the expressed will of Christ as you pray for One.

What occurs when we pray for One is that our entire outlook on life changes. Instead of viewing people as nuisances, we see them as the One. People are no longer our competition or our enemies; they are objects of grace waiting to be found.

This is repentance at its finest. Repent is a wonderful word that means much more than just not sinning. Repent means to adopt a new worldview.

Praying for One will produce a new worldview as you see everything through the lens of Jesus and His mission to seek and save the lost. Scripture instructs us to offer our bodies as living sacrifices to the Lord and to be transformed by the renewing of our minds. When we do this we will know God's good, pleasing, and perfect will. Not only will we know it, we will want it too!

Praying for One will change your foundational purpose for living. Life will suddenly spring to life through the sincerity of this simple prayer. When you want what Jesus wants, life finally makes sense, and the joy of spiritual reproduction consumes you.

As our hearts change, we find that we are not too busy to speak to a neighbor or stay late with a coworker. We find that our heads are up and that we make eye contact with people because we never know who the One will be.

No day is wasted, because we arise in the morning with a true sense of mission and purpose. The first words on our lips are, "Give me One." The gospel becomes each day's destination.

Praying for One puts us into position to be fully used by God. This stuff is addictive. You get that first One and you can't stop. You have to have another and another and another. Kingdom growth becomes exponential. One becomes two, two becomes four, four becomes eight, eight becomes sixteen, and so on, as each of your Ones begins to pray for One too.

Why not start right now?

Let's pray.

"Give me One."

CONFESS

They say that confession is good for the soul.

I'm not exactly sure who "they" are, but I can confirm from personal experience that tremendous freedom is derived from confession.

We tend to store things up in our souls. We pack the good and the bad of life's experiences into our core being. We hoard the good like private, hidden treasures and lock away the bad deep within in hopes of protecting our dirty little secrets.

God designed our souls to be more clearinghouses than storehouses. Experiences come in and are processed. Lessons are learned. Memories are made. Emotions are examined.

An outlet of expression is needed to prevent the soul from becoming overcrowded and bogged down. Confession is God's provision for an uncluttered soul.

There are two primary types of confession. The first is a profession of truth or belief. In Christian circles this is often referred to as a "confession of faith." The second is admitting wrongdoing. This would be the "confession of sin." Both are essential for streamlining the soul to allow for maximum spiritual efficiency.

These two types of confession are represented in the first chapter of 1 John.

> *"That which was from the beginning, which we have heard,*
> *which we have seen with our eyes, which we have looked at*
> *and our hands have touched—this we proclaim concerning*

the Word of life. The life appeared; we have seen it and testify to it, and we proclaim to you the eternal life, which was with the Father and has appeared to us. We proclaim to you what we have seen and heard, so that you also may have fellowship with us. And our fellowship is with the Father and with his Son, Jesus Christ. We write this to make our joy complete.

This is the message we have heard from him and declare to you: God is light; in him there is no darkness at all. If we claim to have fellowship with him and yet walk in the darkness, we lie and do not live out the truth. But if we walk in the light, as he is in the light, we have fellowship with one another, and the blood of Jesus, his Son, purifies us from all sin.

If we claim to be without sin, we deceive ourselves and the truth is not in us. If we confess our sins, he is faithful and just and will forgive us our sins and purify us from all unrighteousness. If we claim we have not sinned, we make him out to be a liar and his word is not in us."

1 John 1:1-10

Regularly confessing the authentic nature of Christianity prevents subtle detours of faith. We proclaim what we have experienced in Christ and confess His goodness, grace, mercy, and love. This type of confession prevents pride by continually making Jesus the focal point of faith.

Likewise, confessing sin delivers us from the fantasyland of holier-than-thou make believe. This allows us to be living testimonies to the ultimate truth we profess. When we acknowledge our sins and trust God to handle them, our souls are released from oppression and are free to dynamically echo God's grace.

Confession demolishes the dams of self-reliance and ego-centric faith so that a raging river of life can run through us. This living water refreshes all who we come in contact with.

We begin with confession because confession is the place to start. It is a first step on the journey toward fruitful Kingdom expansion. Confession sets the stage for an entirely new worldview and ushers in a hope that will never disappoint.

THINK ABOUT IT

1. Write a personal statement of faith. Who is Jesus? Who are you in relation to Him? How has God saved you? What are you saved from? What are you saved for? What purpose does God have for your life?

2. Confess your sins. Write them down. There is power in naming your sins and seeing them written down. Release them onto the paper and hold nothing back. As you confess you will find that the subtler sins of the heart will begin to rise to the surface. These can be the hardest to spot and gain freedom from. Don't stop confessing until you feel that you have emptied yourself completely.

3. How does sin distract us from the mission of Jesus?

4. Have you experienced perversions in Christianity? Write down some of the things that Christians pursue in place of Jesus and His mission.

PRAY ABOUT IT

Begin by confessing your faith in Jesus. Tell God what you believe about Him and what He has done for you. Confess your sins to Him. Ask God to reveal anything that is hidden within your heart. Boldly seek God's purpose for your life and then submit yourself to Him. Ask God to give you One to share His love with.

NOTES:

DISCOVER

There is nothing in life quite as exciting as a genuine "Eureka!" moment.

Humans desire significance and purpose. We search for something of value beyond a temporal existence. It does not require much wisdom to know that earthly riches are an illusion, prosperity is fleeting, and the physical world is in a steady state of decay.

Hope cannot be found in material things, so the search is on.

Finding Jesus is a game changer. A true understanding of the eternal value of knowing Jesus as the Christ, the Son of the Living God, produces passionate life change. There is a new aim and trajectory for existence. Jesus holds ultimate value and all other things and relationships become secondary.
Jesus described this type of "Eureka!" moment like finding hidden treasure.

> *"That which was from the beginning, which we have heard, "The kingdom of heaven is like treasure hidden in a field. When a man found it, he hid it again, and then in his joy went and sold all he had and bought that field.*
> *"Again, the kingdom of heaven is like a merchant looking for fine pearls. When he found one of great value, he went away and sold everything he had and bought it."*
> **Matthew 13:44-46**

There is no speculation involved in these two parables. The man found a hidden treasure. The merchant found a pearl of great value. The discovery was made, but further action was required to possess the treasure. Selling everything to acquire a found treasure of great value is not risky. It is a logical and savvy course of action.

Knowing Jesus is a "Eureka!" moment, but it is not our last. We meet Jesus and surrender everything to His lordship, but there is still a search for significance. Christian people want to know what we are living for. Why are we here? What is the meaning of our continued existence? Why can't we just die and go to Heaven now?

The answer to these questions is found in discovering the essence of God's heart. Jesus described Himself as a shepherd and He told this parable:

> *"Now the tax collectors and sinners were all gathering around to hear Jesus. But the Pharisees and the teachers of the law muttered, 'This man welcomes sinners and eats with them.'*
> *Then Jesus told them this parable: 'Suppose one of you has a hundred sheep and loses one of them. Doesn't he leave the ninety-nine in the open country and go after the lost sheep until he finds it? And when he finds it, he joyfully puts it on his shoulders and goes home. Then he calls his friends and neighbors together and says, 'Rejoice with me; I have found my lost sheep.'' I tell you that in the same way there will be more rejoicing in heaven over one sinner who repents than over ninety-nine righteous persons who do not need to repent.'"*

Luke 15:1-7

The heart of God beats for the One who is lost. He is not willing that any of them perish. He sent His Son to save the world, and when we discover Jesus, we also discover His mission.

19

Praying for One is a "Eureka!" moment because this simple prayer aligns our hearts to God's. We treasure what He treasures and the search for One is on.

When we ask God to give us One to share His love with, we are praying His will into our lives. Pray expectantly and confidently. You have discovered something worth living for.

THINK ABOUT IT

1. When you wake up in the morning, is there a sense of urgency in your relationship with Jesus? Are you eager for what the day might hold in regards to building God's Kingdom? What compels you to get out of bed?

2. Have you had a "Eureka!" moment? Have you found something of great value that altered the course of your life?

3. In your continued search for significance, what do you expect to find?

4. If you pray for One to share God's love with, do you think that He will give you One? How might your life change if your primary objective was to search for the One?

PRAY ABOUT IT

Seek Jesus. Ask Him what His will is. Ask Him to reveal your primary purpose for living. Search for that "Eureka!" moment in Him. Ask God to give you One to share His love with.

NOTES:

REPENT

Repent!

That's right...repent with an exclamation point!

Sadly, most people who see the word repent with an exclamation point think of an angry preacher screaming at them. There is some sort of post-traumatic stress disorder that sends them flashing back to an old-fashioned turn-or-burn sermon. You might have even flinched when you read the word (with the exclamation point) just now.

Repent is not an angry word. It is an exciting word. It is a wonderful word that holds great hope and new beginnings. The exclamation of "Repent!" ought to be done with a smile on the face and happiness in the heart.

Repentance does not merely mean to stop sinning. There is a much richer and fulfilling purpose for the ongoing action of repenting. **Repent means to adopt a new worldview. It provides a new lens for experiencing life and making decisions.**

Most people look at the world through the lens of self. The primary concern is about how situations will impact the individual and his or her personal goals and ambitions. This self-centered attitude is far from satisfying and is completely counter-Christ.

Followers of Jesus are in a continual state of repentance through the renewing of the mind.

"Therefore, I urge you, brothers and sisters, in view of God's mercy, to offer your bodies as a living sacrifice, holy and pleasing to God—this is your true and proper worship. Do not conform to the pattern of this world, but be transformed by the renewing of your mind. Then you will be able to test and approve what God's will is—his good, pleasing, and perfect will."

Romans 12:1-2

Praying for One is active repentance. As you pray for One, your primary desire begins to change. You are moved beyond prayers for self and personal kingdom building. Praying for One takes the focus off of self and puts it onto building Christ's eternal Kingdom.

God's will becomes clear. Confusion is eliminated as you begin to desire what God desires. His good, pleasing, and perfect will is to seek and save the lost. Praying for One thrusts you into the middle of God's will, and life explodes with passion and purpose.

When you pray for One, you will find that you are on the ready. There is an expectancy that comes from praying God's expressed will into your life. Every situation and person will look different to you. You will be asking questions like, "Is this my One?" and "Could this be a pray-for-One moment?"

Every encounter becomes divine as you ask God to move His love through you to others. Praying for One is repentance at its finest.

THINK ABOUT IT

1. Is "repent" a word that you are familiar with? At first glance, what emotions did the word evoke? In light of today's devotion, can you get excited about repenting?

2. Describe your current worldview. How do you process information and make decisions? What are your top three priorities?

3. Carefully examine your prayer life. When you pray, what do you ask for? Are your prayers focused more on self or on building God's Kingdom?

4. How do you think your view of the world would change if Christ's mission were constantly at the forefront of your mind?

PRAY ABOUT IT

Ask God for a new worldview. Ask Him to show you the beauty of repentance. Seek the will of God as you pray about what Jesus desires most. Ask God to give you One to share His love with.

NOTES:

ONCE YOU NAME IT... YOU ARE RESPONSIBLE FOR IT

chapter two

ONCE YOU NAME IT...YOU ARE RESPONSIBLE FOR IT

Praying for One begins with a rather general prayer asking God to give you One person to share His love with. The One could be anyone. This type of praying makes you evangelistically available at all times. You begin to look at everyone differently because they might be the answer to your prayer.

People that you might have otherwise ignored will suddenly have your undivided attention. You will listen for cues and conversational openings that enable you to thoughtfully share the love of Jesus. People are dying to hear about Jesus. As you pray for One, you will be amazed by how open people are to the story of Christ and His love.

Sometimes when praying for One, God will lay a specific name on your heart. Chances are that there is a family member, friend, neighbor, co-worker, etc., in your life who does not yet know Jesus. As you pray for One, you will probably end up praying for someone by name. When a specific name is on your heart, there is a responsibility to share God's love with them.

Praying daily for that person by name will cause you to look at them differently. They will become your One. You will not give up on them. You will not stop praying for them. You will take active steps to repeatedly share Jesus with them. You will feel responsible because you have a divine mission.

One morning, I was in our kitchen serving our three children breakfast. At the time, our oldest daughter Alizah was in the fifth grade, our son Ace was in the first grade, and our youngest daughter Ensley was still a year away from starting kindergarten.

The school year had just begun, and I was quizzing Alizah and Ace about how things were going. I was doing a little rapid fire Q and A with them about their teachers, classmates, subject matter, lunches, recess, and so on. As I was doing this, I realized that Ensley was left out of the conversation.

So I turned to her and said, "And you...you...where did you come from? Who are you? And what are you all about?"

Ensley looked up from her Cocoa Puffs and sat up straight in her chair with an appropriate expression of happy confusion on her face. She had no idea how to answer me, but she was glad to be a part of the conversation. I just stared right into her eyes and waited to see what she would say.

That's when Ace spoke up and said, "Hey, Dad...I hear that once you name them, YOU are responsible for them."

We all laughed together over that strange exchange of words, but I have never forgotten it. God spoke to me that morning through my son. There is profound truth in knowing that once you name something you are responsible for it.

When you name your One, you become responsible for sharing Jesus with that person. There is a calling on your life to be Christ's ambassador to the person you are praying for. Just praying for that person becomes unsatisfactory. You will be compelled to take action. You will ask God to use you to share His love with them. You will go out of your way to spend time with them because you fully expect God to move in a mighty way at any moment.

You feel responsible, and it feels good. You are more than a recipient of Christ's Kingdom, you are a participant in building His Kingdom! The monotony of purposeless living is replaced with passionate responsibility. You will love like you have never loved before as Jesus reveals Himself through you. You will hurt for the person you are praying for. You will cry out to God with unparalleled passion. You will plead for them. You will be responsible.

Responsibility is a powerful thing.

When our youngest child, Ensley, started Kindergarten her brother Ace was in the second grade at the same school. The Kindergarten program was just a half-day and Ensley went to school in the afternoon. Each day, Ensley was dropped off at school just before noon and then she rode the bus home with her big brother when school was finished.

My wife and I were pretty nervous about our baby riding the bus home from school, so we appealed to her big brother Ace to be responsible for her. Ace is an amazing kid. He has a sweet spirit, and he loves his sisters. Ace is gentle, thoughtful, trustworthy, and compassionate…but at that time he was also an eight year old boy. We know that our son can be mischievous and a bit rotten at times. He has that "Dennis the Menace" twinkle in his eyes. He is simultaneously endearing and alarming.

We are not the type of parents who pretend our kids are perfect. We have flawed children, and we like them that way. Stepford kids do not interest us in the least. Our kids have amazing personalities that we are responsible for cultivating. We try to set realistic expectations for them, and for the most part, they rise to the occasion, and sometimes they totally blow us away.

So there we were, Mom and Dad, nervous about our baby riding the bus home from school, so we called on the big brother to be responsible. We were not sure how Ace would respond, so we laid it on pretty thick. We told him to make sure his sister got on the right bus, that she was seated safely for the duration of the journey, and that she got off at the right stop. We explained to Ace that his baby sister could get lost, end up on the wrong bus, or be taken by a stranger.

Ace really seemed to understand the gravity of the situation and how much it meant to his mom and dad that he look out for his little sister. Before the first day of school, we showed Ace where the bus would drop them off. We walked him through how to tell the bus driver that they were together. When school finally started, Ace had a very clear mission, and he was up for the challenge.

It was a special moment, watching Ace and Ensley come off of the bus together on the first day of school. We were nervous, but our fears were put to rest when the bus pulled up and we saw Ace help his baby sister gather her belongings, and then he held her arm as she exited the bus. We were proud parents as they ran over to us to tell us all about their day.

Over the next couple of weeks, we reminded Ace to continue to make sure Ensley got on the right bus, but we were slipping into a routine. My wife and I weren't really nervous any longer. Ace had done a great job of helping his sister (and parents) adjust to a new situation. Everything was moving along normally, then one day something different happened.

I took Ace to school early one morning before going about my day. My wife woke up with a stomach bug and was unable to take Ensley to school. I was stuck in a meeting, so we decided to keep Ensley home. I was able to wrap things up early and went to the bus stop to pick up Ace. It was raining outside, so I waited for him in my car.

When the bus stopped, I saw Ace jump up immediately and head for the doors. He had a very serious look on his face. He locked eyes with me as he stepped off the bus, and he sprinted to my car. Ace threw open the back door and very sternly, seriously, and passionately told me what was going on.

He said, "Dad, Ensley was not on the bus. I don't know where she is. I couldn't find her, and I didn't know what to do. I don't know if she got on the wrong bus, if she is lost, or if someone took her. Dad, I don't know where Ensley is."

By the time he finished, his body was shaking and his lips were quivering. He was ghost-white with fear. Ace did not know where his baby sister was, and he felt responsible.

I reached toward him and said, "Oh, buddy, Ensley is at home. She is safe. Mom was sick today and couldn't take her to school. Ensley is waiting for you to come home and play with her."

Ace burst into tears as he climbed into the car. He sat in his seat and sobbed. Between sobs he said, "You should have told me. You should have let me know that Ensley wouldn't be on the bus."

I promised that we would never do that to him again. My gut was wrenching as I sat there with Ace thinking about what the last twenty minutes of his life were like. He rode that bus all that way home not knowing where his baby sister was. He did the only thing he knew to do. The first chance he had, he ran to his dad and told him that his One was lost.

I never want to forget that moment. There are so many people who are not on the bus yet. They are not safe at home with Jesus. They are lost.

And we are responsible.

It is that simple. Praying for One brings the reality of Christ's mission to your doorstep. When God gives you a name, you can't shake it. You become consumed with sharing God's love, and you plead with the Father for the lost to be found.

You cannot rationalize away your responsibility. You will not try to pass off your calling onto paid clergy members. You will stop making excuses. Your life will have purpose.

Once you name it, you are responsible for it. Pray for One, and go get them.

ANYONE

"God, give me One...ANYONE. I don't care who it is...just give me One." God's love cannot be contained. It must be expressed.

God's love is meant to flow into the heart and out of the heart. It is a raging river of life that cuts across the landscape and refreshes everyone.

When God's love is not expressed, a dam is created and the waters begin to stagnate. People who do not actively share God's love end up with shallow pools of death inside. They are not refreshed nor can they refresh anyone.

God's love is living water. As long as it is flowing, it carries sustenance, energy, and transformational power. When one is connected fully to God's love, there is an urgency to find an outlet of expression. His love cannot be held in. If it is not shared then a disconnection will occur on the other end. We pull away from God when we do not allow His love to flow throw us.

It is impossible to grow in Christ when you are not actively sharing His love with others. A relationship with God is very much a communal experience. Our relational God longs for us to connect to Him and to others. His love is the bond that holds us all together. You cannot love God and not love people.

The story of the woman at the well in John chapter 4 is a great example of how God's love flows. The Samaritan woman Jesus encountered was alone and most likely ostracized from her community because of her life experiences. She received love from Jesus and immediately went and shared that love with anyone who would listen.

"Jesus answered her, 'If you knew the gift of God and who it is that asks you for a drink, you would have asked him and he would have given you living water.'

'Sir,' the woman said, 'you have nothing to draw with and the well is deep. Where can you get this living water? Are you greater than our father Jacob, who gave us the well and drank from it himself, as did also his sons and his livestock?' Jesus answered, 'Everyone who drinks this water will be thirsty again, but whoever drinks the water I give them will never thirst. Indeed, the water I give them will become in them a spring of water welling up to eternal life.'"

John 4:10-14

"Then, leaving her water jar, the woman went back to the town and said to the people, 'Come, see a man who told me everything I ever did. Could this be the Messiah?' They came out of the town and made their way toward him."

John 4:28-30

Living water flows. If you are connected to Jesus, then you are attached to an everlasting supply of love. You will never run out of love. There is no need to store it away or hoard it. Be desperate to share God's love. Plead with Him to give you One…anyone…to share His love with today.

A general prayer for One will put you on high alert for who God might put before you each day. Anyone could be your One. Life gets exciting when you are on the steady lookout for opportunities to express God's love. Pray for One, and living water will flow through you.

THINK ABOUT IT

1. Have you ever seen a stagnant pool of water? How did you react to it? Could you imagine drinking from it or using it to clean and refresh yourself? Describe what you feel when you picture water that is dead.

2. Have you ever put up a dam, blocking the outflow of God's love from your heart? What kinds of attitudes and behaviors create these dams? What is the impact on your relationship with God and others?

3. What do you think about praying for anyone? How could God use that prayer to change the way you look at people?

4. Are you open to sharing God's love with anyone? In what ways could God move you out of your comfort zones by praying this prayer?

PRAY ABOUT IT

Ask God to give you One...ANYONE. Tell Him that you don't care who it is...just ask Him to give you One. Plead with God to destroy every dam you have built so that His love can flow through you like a rushing river of life.

NOTES:

SOMEONE

There is nothing in life quite as exciting as a genuine "Eureka!" Praying for anyOne to share God's love with will always lead you to someOne.

God will lay a specific name on your heart. Chances are that there is a family member, friend, neighbor, co-worker, etc., in your life who does not yet know Jesus. As you pray for One, you will end up praying for someOne by name.

Praying daily for that person by name will cause you to look at him or her differently. That person will become your One. You will not give up on that person. You will not stop praying for that person. You will take active steps to repeatedly share Jesus with that person.

This is simply the nature of God's love. It is universal and personal at the same time. God sent His Son Jesus because He so loved the world. Jesus came to save the world. The global expression of God's love though is revealed through individual encounters. This is why Jesus told stories about a lost sheep, a lost coin, and a lost son. **God is consumed with finding lost people and restoring them to His family One at a time.** Every individual is important, and the search will not cease until all are found.

The focal point of the prodigal son parable in Luke 15 is not the action of a wayward son but the undying love of a father. Sons go wayward. It is what they do. That part of the story is not shocking in the least. The father's response is what would have elicited a reaction from Jesus' audience.

"Jesus continued: 'There was a man who had two sons. The younger one said to his father, "Father, give me my share of the estate." So he divided his property between them.

"Not long after that, the younger son got together all he had, set off for a distant country and there squandered his wealth in wild living. After he had spent everything, there was a severe famine in that whole country, and he began to be in need. So he went and hired himself out to a citizen of that country, who sent him to his fields to feed pigs. He longed to fill his stomach with the pods that the pigs were eating, but no one gave him anything.

"When he came to his senses, he said, "How many of my father's hired servants have food to spare, and here I am starving to death! I will set out and go back to my father and say to him: Father, I have sinned against heaven and against you. I am no longer worthy to be called your son; make me like one of your hired servants." So he got up and went to his father.

"But while he was still a long way off, his father saw him and was filled with compassion for him; he ran to his son, threw his arms around him and kissed him.'"

Luke 15:11-20

The father was looking for his son. He saw him from a long way off and was filled with compassion for him. Just picture a loving father scanning the horizon daily in hopes that his son would eventually return.

When the father spotted his son, he immediately took off running to him. This father was gracious, compassionate, slow to anger, and rich in love. The father in this story is our Heavenly Father. He looks for us, runs to us, and restores us to His family.

The Father never forgets about his lost son and neither should we. As you pray for One, God will give you someOne. He will give you a name that you are to pray for and search for daily. God will fill you with compassion for your One and He will use you to help bring him or her back home.

It may take years of faithful prayer and actively sharing God's love before your One comes home to the Father, but when God gives you someOne you just can't give up.

THINK ABOUT IT

1. Who do you know that is far from God? Who is the first person that comes to mind? Why do you think you thought of that person first? What is special about him or her or about the relationship you have with that person?

2. Have you ever thought that someone was so far from God that he or she would never come back? Have you ever been tempted to write somebody off as so lost that they could never be found? How do you think God feels about such sentiments? How does God want you to feel?

3. How will praying for someOne specifically by name every day change your relationship with that person? What are some ways that God will show His love and compassion through you?

4. How do you think your attitude will change toward your One?

PRAY ABOUT IT

Pray for One...anyOne...but as you do, pay attention to any names that pop into your head. When God gives you someOne, pray for him or her daily by name. Ask others to join you in praying for your One and then be on the steady lookout for opportunities to share God's love.

NOTES:

RESPONSIBLE

Humans are created in God's image and are called to share in His work. In Genesis chapter 1, God gave Adam and Eve authority to rule over His creation. In Genesis chapter 2, God allowed Adam to name every living creature.

> *"Now the LORD God had formed out of the ground all the wild animals and all the birds in the sky. He brought them to the man to see what he would name them; and whatever the man called each living creature, that was its name. So the man gave names to all the livestock, the birds in the sky and all the wild animals."*
>
> **Genesis 2:19-20**

God did the work of creation and then invited man to participate in the creative process. In allowing Adam to name the creation, God bestowed on him authority and responsibility over creation. The old adage is true: "Once you name it, you are responsible for it."

It is kind of like having a stray dog that hangs around your house. You can try to ignore it, but if it sticks around long enough, you will give it a name of some sort. Eventually you will refer to the dog as Dog, Mangy Mutt, Spot, Fluffy, Buster, or some such variation. As soon as you name that dog, you become responsible for it. You will show the dog affection, put out food and water, and try to look for its owner or find it a home.

When parents have a child, one of their very first responsibilities is to name that child. Considerable thought goes into naming a child because names are a big deal. Parents name their children, and then they are responsible for them. No one else gets to name that child, but no one else is as responsible for the child's welfare either.

Something similar happens when we pray for One. In praying a general prayer for God to give you One to share His love with, a specific name will often pop into your head. God will give you the name of someone you know, and this person will become your One.

In addition to your general prayers for One, you will begin to pray specifically for the name or names God gives you. As you pray for people by name daily, you will sense a building responsibility for them. It will dramatically change your relationships and the way you view your Ones.

When God gives you a name, you are responsible for sharing His love with that person. If you do not do it, nobody will. God will call you to do this work, and His call must not be ignored. Sometimes God will give you a name of someone who is outside of your comfort zone. God did this to Peter in Acts chapter 10.

> *"While talking with him, Peter went inside and found a large gathering of people. He said to them: 'You are well aware that it is against our law for a Jew to associate with or visit a Gentile. But God has shown me that I should not call anyone impure or unclean. So when I was sent for, I came without raising any objection. May I ask why you sent for me?'*
>
> *Cornelius answered: 'Three days ago I was in my house praying at this hour, at three in the afternoon. Suddenly a man in shining clothes stood before me and said, "Cornelius, God has heard your prayer and remembered your gifts to the poor. Send to Joppa for Simon who is called Peter. He is a guest in the home of Simon the tanner, who lives by the sea." So I sent for you immediately, and it was good of you to come. Now we are all here in the presence of God to listen to everything the Lord has commanded you to tell us.'"*
>
> **Acts 10:27-33**

God sent Peter to Cornelius. It went against everything Peter had ever known to go to Cornelius' house to share God's love with him. Cornelius was a Gentile and Peter was a Jew. God was working on the hearts of both men at the same time. The same thing happens when we pray for One. God prepares our hearts to go and share, and He prepares the hearts of our Ones to receive.

When God gives us specific names, He will also provide opportunities for His love to flow through us. We are responsible for being open, ready, and available to share God's love with the names He gives us.

THINK ABOUT IT

1. Have you ever given a name or even a nickname to a person? In what ways did you feel more responsible for him or her after giving the name? Think about family members, friends, etc., to whom you have given a name. What do the names you gave them reveal about your relationships with them?

2. Who is God laying on your heart to share His love with? What fears do you have about being responsible for sharing God's love with that person?

3. What are some obstacles or barriers that might get in the way of God's love moving through you to that person?

4. How do you think praying for One will prepare your heart and the One's heart? Are you willing to take action to share God's love with any name He may give you? How do you think praying for specific names will change your relationships with those people?

PRAY ABOUT IT

Ask God to give you One to share His love with. Be still and silent. Listen to discover specific names God will give you. Pray for the names God gives you daily, and aggressively look for opportunities to share His love with your Ones.

NOTES:

ENTRUSTED

Christians are not just recipients of God's grace; we are also participants in sharing His grace. God entrusts us with the greatest treasure imaginable. He saves us by His grace and then puts us to work as distributors of His grace.

> *"For it is by grace you have been saved, through faith— and this is not from yourselves, it is the gift of God— not by works, so that no one can boast. For we are God's handiwork, created in Christ Jesus to do good works, which God prepared in advance for us to do."*
>
> **Ephesians 2:8-10**

There are specific things that God has prepared for us to do. If we fail to do those things, then they will remain undone. The gravity of what is entrusted to us is immense. Praying for One prepares the mind for action so that we are able to recognize the good works God has prepared for us to do.

We are entrusted with the mission of Jesus. As His Church, we must continue His work of seeking and saving the lost. If we do not do it, then nobody will. The stakes are high and eternity hangs in the balance.

Jesus told a parable to describe how we are entrusted with the greatest riches of the Kingdom of Heaven.

> *"Again, it will be like a man going on a journey, who called his servants and entrusted his wealth to them. To one he gave five bags of gold, to another two bags, and to another one bag, each according to his ability. Then he went on his journey. The man who had received five bags of gold went at once and put his money to work and gained five bags more. So also, the one with two bags of gold gained two more. But*

the man who had received one bag went off, dug a hole in the ground and hid his master's money.

"After a long time the master of those servants returned and settled accounts with them. The man who had received five bags of gold brought the other five. 'Master,' he said, 'you entrusted me with five bags of gold. See, I have gained five more.'

"His master replied, 'Well done, good and faithful servant! You have been faithful with a few things; I will put you in charge of many things. Come and share your master's happiness!'

"The man with two bags of gold also came. 'Master,' he said, 'you entrusted me with two bags of gold; see, I have gained two more.'

"His master replied, 'Well done, good and faithful servant! You have been faithful with a few things; I will put you in charge of many things. Come and share your master's happiness!'

"Then the man who had received one bag of gold came. 'Master,' he said, 'I knew that you are a hard man, harvesting where you have not sown and gathering where you have not scattered seed. So I was afraid and went out and hid your gold in the ground. See, here is what belongs to you.'

"His master replied, 'You wicked, lazy servant! So you knew that I harvest where I have not sown and gather where I have not scattered seed? Well then, you should have put my money on deposit with the bankers, so that when I returned I would have received it back with interest. So take the bag of gold from him and give it to the one who has ten bags. For whoever has will be given more, and they will have an abundance. Whoever does not have, even what they have will be taken from them. And throw that worthless servant outside, into the darkness, where there will be weeping and gnashing of teeth."

Matthew 25:14-30

A day of judgment awaits all humankind. On that day we must give an account for what was entrusted to us. The good and faithful servants doubled what was entrusted to them, but the wicked and lazy servant merely protected what he was responsible for.

Our salvation is not meant to be buried deep inside to be protected from worldly contamination. Salvation is a treasure that must be shared and multiplied. There are many who claim to know Christ but have zero understanding of the implications of authentic faith. Out of fear, they bury their treasure and squander their real purpose for living.

The primary reason so many churchgoers are miserable is because they are not actively investing in the Kingdom of Heaven. They sit around waiting for Jesus to come, while the world He so desperately loves remains lost and separated from Him.

You are God's handiwork. You are entrusted with the greatest treasure the world has ever known. Pray for One and do not waste your faith.

THINK ABOUT IT

1. Have you ever been entrusted with a great responsibility? How does knowing that God has prepared good works for you to do make you feel?

2. Think about the story that Jesus told about the workers who were entrusted with different amounts of their master's money. Which of those workers actions most clearly represent how you have invested in God's Kingdom? What are some ways that your attitudes must change in order for you to grow as a faithful servant of Jesus?

3. Faith in Jesus is not a hidden treasure. It is to be shared and multiplied. Do you sense the enormity of the mission you are entrusted with? What are some ways that people try to diminish the responsibility Christians have to share their faith?

4. How do you think praying for One can change those attitudes?

PRAY ABOUT IT

Thank God for the new life He has given you in Christ Jesus. Spend some time praising Him for giving you purpose and meaning. Ask God to prepare you for action so that you will complete every good work He intends for you to do. Pray for One and invest in the Kingdom of Heaven.

NOTES:

EXPERTLY
COMPLICATED

chapter three

EXPERTLY COMPLICATED

How did Christianity get so complicated?

Jesus entrusted His Church to a group of ordinary, unschooled people who believed so deeply in His mission that they died for Him. They were so busy sharing the simple gospel that there was no time to make it complex. The Lord was adding to their number daily those who were being saved.

Many subtle shifts have occurred over the centuries. Christianity became a state religion. It was organized. Church became big business. Power struggles ensued. The mission was sometimes lost.

But Jesus has never given up on His Church. He has bet all of eternity on the Church. We are His plan A, and there is no plan B. With all of our failings, the Church still prevails as the light of the world. Light is a very simple thing. It either shines or it doesn't. The same is true for the Church.

The light of the Church is shining brightly. Worldwide there are more people coming to know Jesus as Lord and Savior today than at any other time in history. The gospel is booming! The question we must wrestle with is: Are we a part of this explosion of light?

I am a pastor. I am a part of a system that can profit from making simple truths complex. I admit that I have desired to be a part of the system of "religious experts." I have tried to finagle my way into the club, but one requirement continually trips me up. I can't get my head around taking the simple truth of Jesus and making it inaccessible to others. The whole notion of "religious experts" runs contrary to the beauty of the gospel.

Seriously? Religious experts? What does that even mean?

Do you want to know who the real religious experts are in practicing true religion? It is not necessarily the highly-educated, professional clergy, authors, speakers, and pop-culture Jesus icons. The religious experts are the ones who excel at taking care of orphans and widows in their distress. Religious experts have a childlike faith that is accompanied by obedient action. Experts in following Jesus demonstrate their faith in abiding love for God that is reproduced exponentially as they generously share the hope that they possess.

The church I serve with is in Manchester, New Hampshire. We have some of the greatest religious experts I have ever encountered. The people of Manchester Christian Church pray for One, and that simple prayer has driven them to deep action. There was a small group of people in our church that became aware of a problem in our city. On Saturdays and Sundays, there were no shelters or services providing breakfast for our homeless neighbors. Their love for Jesus compelled them to act.

Once they recognized the need, they began showing up at a downtown park with breakfast foods. They shared a meal, a devotional thought, and the love of Jesus with anyone who wanted to join them. Initially, they served a "cold" breakfast, but they were not content with that. The Holy Spirit stirred within them to give their best, so they began to cook hot, delicious food. Word spread quickly.

They created a ministry named "Do You Know Him?" because their ultimate goal is for everyone to know Jesus. In less than one year, the ministry grew to over 150 regular volunteers who help serve hundreds of people each Saturday and Sunday morning. People aren't just eating a meal, they are being saved.

An older lady who helped start the ministry came up to me one Sunday and said, "Oh, honey, I prayed for ONE and got 22. What do I do now?" I replied, "Well, what do you want to do?" She looked at me with tears in her eyes and a grin on her face and said, "I want to pray for another One!"

This ministry changed the complexion of our church as our doors were suddenly thrown open to an entirely new demographic of people. The social, economic, and racial diversity is beautiful. We worship together. We serve together. We laugh together. We cry together. Most importantly, we are together. There is no "us" and "them"…it's all us. We are Manchester Christian Church.

Our church has grown so much that, out of necessity, we opened new campuses. We ran out of seats. There was nowhere left to put people. We started a beautiful new campus downtown that is within walking distance from the park where breakfast is served. Now everyone can come without having to catch a ride. But our Downtown Campus is not a homeless church. It is Manchester

Christian Church. It is that same beautiful mixture of people. We are experiencing heaven on earth.

This is what happens when you move beyond the academics of Christianity and into the reality of being a disciple of Jesus. Discipleship is simple, but simple does not mean shallow. In fact, the simplest things are often the deepest. Our religious experts pray for One and are radically obedient to the mission of Christ. The world is in desperate need of more people who are experts in true religion.

A religious expert is really just a disciple, and a disciple is really just a follower of Jesus. What do followers of Jesus do? They do what Jesus did. Jesus was asked why He came to earth, and He replied, "The Son of Man came to seek and save the lost."

The professional Christian community is perpetually tempted to promote myths regarding discipleship. Complexity creates job security because people must rely on experts to instruct them. The average churchgoer has no hope of interpreting the intricate system of expectations and regulations that are invented by men. The burden of the complex system proves to be too much as the weight of law crushes people and prevents them from following Jesus. What remains is a stagnant mess of defeated despair.

Everyone who receives the good news of Jesus starts out the same. We want to share His extraordinary love with others. We want more people in the Kingdom of Heaven, but then something happens. We hit a snag. There's a bump in the road. There's push back and spiritual attack. Without realizing it, we adjust our initial aim and shoot for something that produces less resistance.

These new goals and objectives are usually good and often even noble. They are easy to support from scripture. Churchy people like the sound of them and eagerly nod their approval. They gain traction quickly and produce a minor spark of life and hope.

The problem with these new goals is that they are not what Jesus called us to do. We share in His mission, and when Jesus was asked what He came here to do, He did not mince any words. Jesus said that the Son of Man came to seek and save the lost. So if a church is not seeking and saving the lost, it is not fulfilling the mission of Jesus and, by definition, is not a church.

The temptation is to throw around weird little phrases like, "We are equipping the saints." Ok, but what in the world are you equipping the saints to do? It better be to seek and save the lost because that is what Jesus commanded. What good are more saintly saints if they aren't fulfilling the mission of Jesus? They are no good. They are a waste of Jesus with skin on. What good are they serving if Jesus is not actively demonstrating His love through them? Jesus warned us that fruitless branches would be cut off.

What are Christians?

They are resources.

Resources for what?

To seek and save the lost!

To live is Christ, and to die is gain. If we live, it is to carry out the purpose of Jesus' life on earth. We will have an eternity to worship Jesus and to know Him fully, but the here and now is the only opportunity we have to seek and save the lost. We don't get to do that in eternity, so we better leverage every resource at our disposal right now to make sure that every single lost one is found. We do not rest, stop, or pause until the mission is complete.

Some will argue that we are out of our minds. BINGO! We are out of our minds for Christ. We are starting to get over personal agendas, insecurities, and selfishness. Love us. Hate us.

We don't care. We just want you to love Jesus and snatch others from the eternal fire of Hell.

Some will say that we are too focused on evangelism. Think about that for a minute. Seriously consider the implications of that statement. How can Christ's Church ever be too focused on His mission? It is absurd to think that we could ever go overboard when it comes to seeking and saving the lost.

On Judgment Day, I can't imagine Jesus condemning us for trying too hard to seek the lost. I doubt that we will be chastised for lovingly proclaiming the beauty of the simple gospel with focused clarity instead of muddling through confusion-invoking studies on irrelevant subject matter.

Some may say, "Well, it is Jesus who saves, not us."

True, but what exactly do you think that the Church is? We are the body of Christ. We are His physical presence here on earth. It is extremely difficult to philosophize and explain away the Great Commission.

The apostles and the early Church gave their lives for the simple gospel. Persecution and the critical nature of the mission prevented perverting the gospel with false notions of easy living or new and improved strands of legalism. Seeking and saving the lost was paramount. That simple mission remains, and the Church must take hold of it.

Do you want to see a change? Pray for One, and watch what happens. Nothing remains the same when we pray for One. I believe with all my heart that one simple prayer can change the landscape of the modern church, the world, and your life.

"God, please give me One person to share your love with today. Amen."

LIGHT

Light is one of the most powerful forces in the universe. It conquers darkness, reveals what is hidden, and drives out fear. Light shows the way and reveals the truth.

Light is only useful when it shines. Hidden lights are wasted energy. Denying our darkened world the light it desperately desires is despicable and disobedient. If the light of Jesus is in you, you are responsible for allowing it to shine.

> *"You are the light of the world. A town built on a hill cannot be hidden. Neither do people light a lamp and put it under a bowl. Instead they put it on its stand, and it gives light to everyone in the house. In the same way, let your light shine before others, that they may see your good deeds and glorify your Father in heaven."*
>
> **Matthew 5:14-16**

Christians often speak about the differences between religion and relationship.

Religion is typically a structured system of rules and practices that participants navigate in attempt to please their god. Religious experiences are often steeped in tradition and ritual. These practices are foreign to outsiders and can become barriers to evangelistic endeavors. In essence, when religion is the focus, it can actually hide the light instead of magnifying the light.

The relational reality of knowing Jesus removes religious barriers and allows light to shine freely and brightly. The intimidation and competition that religious environments promote are destroyed through the opportunity to have a dynamic, growing relationship with the Creator. People are easily tripped up by the complexity of religious systems, but the concept of a relationship is something anyone can grasp.

Since all people are different, the individual expressions of relationship will have unique qualities. When we actively create and foster environments for dynamic relationships with Jesus to flourish, His light is magnified within us. People are attracted to the light. They are drawn to people who are alive with hope, purpose, and love.

Christians are relationally connected to God through the lordship of Jesus. While the relationship is indeed personal, it is never meant to be private. An authentic relationship with Jesus demands an outlet for expression. The human heart becomes a beacon of light when it is filled with the love of Jesus.

Jesus declared that you are the light of the world. If you do not shine, then darkness will prevail. This cannot be!

Accept the simple reality of who you are in Christ. Reject any religious sensibilities that you have allowed to shade the light of Jesus. **Allow God to strip away every shred of shady behavior so that His light can burst freely from you.**

Light is only good if it shines. What good are we doing the Kingdom of Heaven if we refuse to shine before others? How will they ever know Jesus if we allow them to remain in darkness?

Praying for One fixes our minds on our purpose and mission. When our primary objective is to share God's love with others, we stop defending the elements of our lives that block the light of Jesus. We are then free to shine and show others the way.

THINK ABOUT IT

1. It is easy to take light for granted. You can flip on a light switch without any thought to how much you depend on the light. What do you love about light? In what ways do you depend on light? Describe the power of light and how you utilize it daily.

2. What are the ramifications of Jesus declaring that you are the light of the world? Do you picture yourself as a city on a hill? Are you a place of refuge that people are drawn to for answers and hope? How can having the proper perspective on who you are in Christ change how others are able to experience Christ through you?

3. In what ways have you allowed the light of Christ to be hidden in you? Have you tried to keep your relationship with Jesus a private matter?

4. Do you have any religious tendencies that repel people instead of inviting them toward Jesus? What sin have you allowed to shade the light that is in you?

PRAY ABOUT IT

Ask God to remove anything that is blocking His light from shining within you. Seek a dynamic relationship with Jesus that magnifies His light and attracts others. Pray for One and make necessary sacrifices to be the light of the world.

NOTES:

EXPERTS

Expertise is a valuable commodity. Experts are generally sought after, revered, honored, set apart, and held in high esteem. Most people strive to achieve in their given fields because expertise is rewarding. It often brings financial gains, respect, and power.

Organized religion is not different in this regard. Jesus had much to say to the religious experts of His day, and most of it was not flattering. One of His chief complaints about the Pharisees was that they complicated the Law and placed heavy burdens on the people.

This is why Jesus said:

> *"Come to me, all you who are weary and burdened, and I will give you rest. Take my yoke upon you and learn from me, for I am gentle and humble in heart, and you will find rest for your souls. For my yoke is easy and my burden is light."*

Matthew 11:28-30

A relationship with Jesus is not cumbersome or complicated. It is a simple affair that anyone can understand and excel in. Jesus came to remove obstacles that prevent people from connecting to God. One such obstacle is the faulty notion that expertise in following Him is achieved through navigating an ever-growing complexity of rites, rituals, and religious mumbo-jumbo.

The New Testament book of James is essentially a summary of Jesus' teachings. It is a fantastically straightforward book that is easy to understand and apply. It defines religious expertise in this way:

"Do not merely listen to the word, and so deceive yourselves. Do what it says. Anyone who listens to the word but does not do what it says is like someone who looks at his face in a mirror and, after looking at himself, goes away and immediately forgets what he looks like. But whoever looks intently into the perfect law that gives freedom, and continues in it—not forgetting what they have heard, but doing it—they will be blessed in what they do.

"Those who consider themselves religious and yet do not keep a tight rein on their tongues deceive themselves, and their religion is worthless. Religion that God our Father accepts as pure and faultless is this: to look after orphans and widows in their distress and to keep oneself from being polluted by the world."

James 1:22-27

True religious experts have a childlike faith that is accompanied by obedient action. They excel at demonstrating God's love without regard for reciprocation. The allure of earthly reward lacks luster because the Kingdom being built is not of this world.

As we strive toward expertise in following Jesus, may it be with a growing sense of simplistic conviction. Praying for One strips away the hierarchy and competitive nature of organized religion by leveling the playing field. Every Christian is a valuable participant in building God's Kingdom. Advanced academic degrees, fancy titles, and various vestments are not the calling cards of Jesus-following experts. God's love flowing unencumbered is the mark of authentic disciples. They will know us by our love.

THINK ABOUT IT

1. When you think of religious experts, what comes to mind? What similarities do you see between the religious experts of Jesus' day and what Christianity has evolved into today?

2. Describe what you think life looks like for authentic Jesus following experts. What evidence should exist to demonstrate ever-growing devotion to Jesus and His Kingdom-building work?

3. How does knowing that you can (and should) be an expert in following Jesus impact you? Do you feel empowered?

4. What lingering doubts do you have regarding how God intends to use you to build His Kingdom?

PRAY ABOUT IT

Ask God what He thinks about you. Spend some time prayerfully reflecting on how you can be an expert in sharing God's love. Pray for One and commit yourself to allowing God's love to flow through you.

NOTES:

SIMPLE

Simple does not mean shallow, and complex does not mean deep.

There is a fallacy in religious circles that promotes complexity as a pathway to spiritual depth. This type of thinking flies in the face of Jesus' teachings about childlike faith. Jesus warns us that unless we become like little children, we will not inherit the Kingdom of God.

> *"And he said: 'Truly I tell you, unless you change and become like little children, you will never enter the kingdom of heaven.'"*
>
> **Matthew 18:3**

There is a temptation to complicate simple matters. Sometimes this is done so that there can be an excuse for disobedience. If we claim that we cannot understand something then how can we be held accountable for not doing it? Pride is another driving force for complicating simple matters. Many complex systems of thought have developed based primarily on the premise of establishing some sort of power or control.

The Pharisees of Jesus' day certainly fell victim to this type of thinking. Jesus was often harsh in His dealings with these experts of the Law. He scolded them for weighing down the people with heavy burdens of complex nonsense. The religious system was so full of rules, regulations, interpretations, adaptations, and misinformation that it was impossible for anyone to navigate.

People were lost. Jesus said that they were like sheep without a shepherd. They had no hope and could not connect relationally with God. Jesus called people to Himself and into a simple relationship that would allow for tremendous depth.

> *"Come to me, all you who are weary and burdened, and I will give you rest. Take my yoke upon you and learn from me, for I am gentle and humble in heart, and you will find rest for your souls. For my yoke is easy and my burden is light."*
>
> **Matthew 11:28-30**

Sadly, much of today's Christianity has moved away from the simple beauty of knowing Jesus and into the shallow pools of religious complexity. Academics replace obedience. Knowledge overrides love. Pompousness drives out humility. Judgment belies grace.

Returning to the simple beauty of Christ's mission makes Jesus accessible to everyone. Jesus said, "Let the little children come to me and do not hinder them because the Kingdom of Heaven belongs to them."

Praying for One restores us to a childlike faith that allows for limitless depth.

When our primary desire is to see more people in the Kingdom of Heaven, we press hard after Jesus. Praying for One connects the dots between loving God, loving people, and inviting others to know Him. There is transformational depth in this simple prayer. It aligns your heart with God's and provides a simple worldview to guide you in following Jesus.

Simple does not mean shallow. In fact, simple is a depth driver. If you long to go deeper in your relationship with Jesus, keep it simple!

THINK ABOUT IT

1. What are some ways you have seen Christianity morph into a complex religious system instead of a dynamic growing relationship?

2. Describe what you think childlike faith in Jesus looks like. How would you express that kind of faith?

3. How can you be a maturing believer in Jesus while remaining childlike?

4. Are you ever tempted to complicate Christianity? Why do you think people are tempted to turn the simplicity of knowing Jesus and making Him known into a complicated mess?

PRAY ABOUT IT

Ask God to help you keep it simple. Prayerfully seek to discover any ways in which you have complicated your relationship with Jesus. Pray for One and commit yourself to the simple mission of Christ.

NOTES:

PURPOSE

Jesus came to seek and save the lost.

His purpose is clear. Regardless of your personal feelings on evangelism and the nature of the evangelical church, the mission of Jesus remains the same. It will not change until every single One is found and restored to the Father.

Consider our most famous verse of scripture. You know what I am referring to. You have seen it at sporting events, heard it in countless sermons, and probably even memorized some version of John 3:16.

> *"For God so loved the world that he gave his one and only Son, that whoever believes in him shall not perish but have eternal life. For God did not send his Son into the world to condemn the world, but to save the world through him."*
> **John 3:16-17**

The Father sent His son Jesus to earth to save the world. Jesus came to save the world. The purpose of Jesus is to save the world.

After Jesus' death, burial, and resurrection, He ascended into Heaven and left His Church here to continue His mission. Jesus gave us His Holy Spirit to empower us to do His work. The Holy Spirit provides supernatural gifts and spiritual fruit to everyone He indwells. The purpose of the gifts and the fruit is to advance the mission of Christ's Church.

It is imperative that we refrain from squandering these precious resources by wasting them on anything other than the pursuit of Christ's purpose. God's heart beats for the One who is lost. When we pray for One, we intentionally align ourselves with

God's will and get in rhythm with His Spirit. **A passionate, unstoppable desire to find Ones who are far from God drives us deeper into a transforming relationship with the Creator. We want what He wants, and our only ambition is to fulfill His purpose.**

In Luke 19, Jesus had an encounter that reveals His heart for Ones who are lost.

> *"Jesus entered Jericho and was passing through. A man was there by the name of Zacchaeus; he was a chief tax collector and was wealthy. He wanted to see who Jesus was, but because he was short he could not see over the crowd. So he ran ahead and climbed a sycamore-fig tree to see him, since Jesus was coming that way.*
>
> *When Jesus reached the spot, he looked up and said to him, 'Zacchaeus, come down immediately. I must stay at your house today.' So he came down at once and welcomed him gladly.*
>
> *All the people saw this and began to mutter, 'He has gone to be the guest of a sinner.'*
>
> *But Zacchaeus stood up and said to the Lord, 'Look, Lord! Here and now I give half of my possessions to the poor, and if I have cheated anybody out of anything, I will pay back four times the amount.'*
>
> *Jesus said to him, 'Today salvation has come to this house, because this man, too, is a son of Abraham. For the Son of Man came to seek and to save the lost.'"*
>
> **Luke 19:1-10**

Mutter as they may, the delusional and self-righteous cannot change the purpose of Jesus. Jesus came to seek and save the lost. The Church is the body of Christ and we remain on earth to fulfill His mission. The Church's every endeavor ought to be connected to our ultimate purpose.

Praying for One connects the dots between growing in Christ and growing Christ's Kingdom. They always go hand in hand, and you cannot have one without the other. Disciples make disciples when disciples do what Jesus did.

THINK ABOUT IT

1. What do you think about those people who "muttered" about Jesus going to the house of a sinner? Why do you think they were confused?

2. Have you ever witnessed or participated in similar muttering?

3. Does your personal ambition align with Christ's purpose? Do you want what God wants? What are some goals and desires that pull you away from doing God's will?

4. Can you connect the dots between growing in Christ and growing Christ's Kingdom? How is God doing this in you?

PRAY ABOUT IT

Ask God to make His purpose your greatest ambition. Align yourself with God's will by praying for One. Ask God to make His greatest desire your greatest desire and commit yourself to live for His purpose.

NOTES:

THE COST OF FREE

chapter four

THE COST OF FREE

Grace is free, but discipleship will cost you everything.

Identity is the only thing of value that we possess.

Money is an illusion. It's just a bunch of made up numbers. None of it is real. Each month numbers show up in the bank account, then they go away. Hope in economic security is about as real as sitting on a cloud.

Possessions have zero eternal value. They will all pass away. The heavens and the earth will all disappear. Along with your house, car, golf clubs, clothes, and jewelry. If you try to hold onto them, you'll just share in their destruction.

Families fail. Divorce, death, and dysfunction destroy families. If your family is your ultimate, you will ultimately be disappointed.

The only thing Jesus wants is you.

Jesus calls us to be His disciples, but discipleship is one of those churchy words that gets manipulated and twisted in all sorts of deceptive ways. Discipleship often gets relegated into classes and programs that focus on knowledge transference.

The general thinking is that the more we learn, the more we will be like Jesus. Practical experience should have demolished this myth long ago, but we still gladly replace following Jesus with biblical stuffiness. The Bible is abused like food for a glutton. Instead of fuel for the mission, the scriptures become addictive junk food. The Bible is abused like a drug as we grow puffed up, lethargic, and obese. The mission of following Jesus gets replaced with the drive to be smarter than the rest.

We are forced to turn inward in efforts to justify the absence of evangelistic traction. Instead of talking about, dreaming of, and praying over people getting saved, we argue about petty nuances of scripture that are largely irrelevant. Christians divide over the ridiculous. The Bible is used as a weapon against one another instead of as a sword to set the captives free.

Don't get me wrong. I love the Bible. I read it every day. I preach from it every Sunday. I memorize scripture, and I encourage everyone to seek Jesus in all sixty-six wonderful books.

But, I do not worship the Bible. I worship Jesus. Discipleship is following Jesus.

We cannot replace following Jesus with following the Bible. In order for the Bible to be useful for discipleship, it must be read through the lens of Jesus. We must consider who Jesus is and His mission before we can appropriately apply scripture to daily living. If we fail to do this, then scripture will be taken out of context and abused for whatever purpose we deem desirable.

At the extreme level, you can picture those protesters that we have all seen on television holding up signs that say things like "God hates fags." Those devils are the worst kind of Antichrist. They misrepresent who Jesus is because of a perverted agenda. But is it possible that we participate in the same kind of activity every time we use the Bible for something other than an encounter with the living, loving Jesus?

Hopefully the thought of misrepresenting Jesus to this lost, broken, and devastated world disturbs you greatly. My heart breaks over the vast amount of resources that are wasted on false discipleship efforts. The enemy's number one tactic is to get the Church to focus on anything other than the mission of Jesus. If he can get us to fight on a false front, then he wins the battle no matter how valiantly or powerfully we struggle. Fighting the wrong fight is actually worse than not fighting at all.

For years now, I have read books and listened to Christian leaders discuss and debate over what authentic discipleship looks like. I have encountered countless discipleship models, programs, and strategies. They all seek to create a measurable system where growth can be documented and compared. We have complicated the simplest of concepts in attempts to control and contain what can only be a dynamic experience. Discipleship is not something you can conquer and graduate from. It is a journey that leads into eternity. We do not arrive as disciples of Jesus until we fall at His feet at judgment and experience His refining fire once and for all.

We must refrain from removing the mystery and wonder of following Jesus. It is a glorious thing to stumble after the Messiah. The Bible is full of flawed people who pursued God and sometimes succeeded but often failed. Discipleship is nothing other than following Jesus and doing what He did.

Jesus was crystal clear on what following Him would look like. The central components of His teachings reveal three indicative marks that every follower of Christ will exhibit. Authentic disciples love God, love people, and reproduce spiritually. These are the marks of Kingdom-minded men and women. They are consumed with love and purpose. The allure of this world and the distractions of self are no match for the compelling nature of following hard after Jesus. Authentic disciples have tasted the heavenly gift of living beyond this realm, and there is no satisfaction in the purely temporal.

When Jesus was asked what the greatest commandment is, He replied: "Love the Lord your God with all your heart, soul, mind, and strength." Love is discipleship fuel. When someone is connected to God through a relationship with Jesus, they are able to receive and reciprocate love. The love of God is more than the human heart can contain, so it bursts out and overflows in a sort of love explosion.

The most important thing is to love God with every fiber of your being. Hold nothing back. Nothing is off limits to Him. You are to love God with all of your heart, soul, mind, and strength. This reveals to us the all-encompassing nature of discipleship. There are no partial disciples. Either you are all in, or you aren't in at all. This notion ought to disturb and shake us at our very core. Christianity is not a child's play thing. Jesus is not to be toyed with. The thought of merely playing follow the leader with Jesus until we become bored, tired, afraid, or irritated is a vulgar concept indeed!

There are no vacations from discipleship. We are never on a break from God. Compartmentalization is a lie. Thinking that we can effectively follow Jesus in one area of our life while deliberately disobeying Him in another area is insane. We attempt to barter and compromise, but God does not compromise. His terms are clear. Love Him with everything you have.

Our God is a jealous God. He will not share us. He is unwilling to accept idolatry. We can get sucked into the vicious world of idolatry without much awareness at all. Our idols are often good things that become supreme things. We put them ahead of God and allow them to dictate our thoughts and actions. Family, work, recreation, health, prosperity, nationalism, humanistic endeavors, and so on, can easily become the primary filters that drive our lives.

The command to love the Lord your God with all of your heart, soul, mind, and strength does not allow for any form of idolatry. God is faithful in this command by allowing us to receive salvation with our whole being. Acts 2 recounts the story of the first time the gospel of Jesus was shared with a group of people. Their response is telling.

When they heard the message of Jesus, they were cut to the heart and said, "What must we do to be saved?" Peter replied, "Repent and be baptized, every one of you, in the name of Jesus Christ for the forgiveness of your sins."

Salvation is a holistic experience.

The people heard the story of Jesus and were cut to the heart. The love of God hit them at their core. This is the initial response to an awareness of God's intense love for us. We receive it in our hearts, and the heart/soul cannot contain it. We are compelled to action because the love of God requires release.

The people asked, "What must we do to be saved?"

For the sake of a theological side note, it is important to state that salvation is not initiated by our actions. Ephesians 2:8-10 reminds us that, "For it is by grace you have been saved, through faith—and this not from yourselves, it is the gift of God— not by works, so that no one can boast. For we are God's workmanship, created in Christ Jesus to do good works, which God prepared in advance for us to do."

I have no desire to get sidetracked by a debate regarding the nature of grace and works in the salvation process. I would also prefer to avoid triggering the various defenses about what is required for salvation. For the most part, that discussion simply detracts from the beauty of Christ's redemptive work. Attempts to ascertain the bare minimum requirements for salvation reveal a lack of understanding of lordship. Salvation is only found through Jesus being Lord. If Jesus is Lord, then obedience will follow. Salvation opens the door for obedience to all of God's commands through a relationship with Jesus. The truly saved person has no reason to balk at any of God's commands.

So, back to the question that was asked in Acts chapter 2. "What must we do to be saved?"

The Apostle Peter replied, "Repent and be baptized, every one of you, in the name of Jesus Christ for the forgiveness of your sins."

Already, they were cut to the heart. The jealous love of God was pounding on and in their hearts and souls. They were desperate to respond, and Peter told them to do two things.

The first was to repent. Receiving grace, forgiveness, and salvation all begins with one of the greatest words ever...Repent. Repentance is far more than feeling bad or sorry for sinning. It is more than making a commitment to try not to sin anymore. Repentance entails a completely fresh and new start. It is a choice to have your entire worldview changed.

Romans 12:2 says, "Be transformed by the renewing of

your mind." Repentance means that we get to live for God instead of anything else. Repentance means that the number one, most important thing in our lives is our relationship with God. Repentance means that we are restored to the place God intended for us to be from the beginning...to an interdependent relationship with our loving Creator.

The new way of thinking that comes from repentance provides a fresh outlook on life as we experience the love of God with our minds. The only way to love God with all your mind is through repentance. We take captive every thought and make it obedient to Christ by filtering it through an eternal view of salvation. As this occurs, our internal dialogue begins to change. Our passions, desires, and dreams are altered by a radically different vision of what the future holds. We start to want what God wants as our minds are captured by His graceful promptings. The temporal loses its grip as our thoughts are consumed with matters of eternal significance.

The second way Peter told them to respond was to be baptized. Baptism is the physical experience connected to the emotional and mental surrender to Jesus. The command to be baptized should not be surprising. Jesus was baptized. He commanded His disciples to "go and baptize." There is no reason for anyone who has been cut to the heart with the gospel and is experiencing the transforming of the mind through repentance not to be baptized.

Sadly though, baptism has landed on the denominational battle lines. It has been fought over, abused, neglected, and misrepresented for centuries. The mere mention of it causes some to shut down completely.

It saddens me greatly when baptism is argued about and debated. I believe that we clearly have missed the entire point of baptism when it becomes little more than a "doctrinal issue" that must be proved. I have never once met a Christ-follower who refused baptism after hearing about the true beauty of the sacred experience. I have, however, met many who, after taking their doctrinal beating, refused baptism because it had become merely a theological point to be proved.

Baptism is one of God's greatest gifts to His children. It is commanded clearly in scripture and was part of the normative conversion/initiation practice in the early Church. That alone should be sufficient reason to be baptized. The issue generally becomes contentious when we discuss what actually occurs at the point of baptism.

Does the Holy Spirit come at baptism? Does salvation occur at baptism? Are sins washed away at baptism?

The point is not to understand fully what transpires at baptism but to respond in obedience to the command. In the book of Acts, we see several different conversion experiences with different things happening at different times. This leads to some of the confusion and provides ammunition for the doctrinal debate. The debates are a distraction from the beauty of the gift of baptism. The fact is that God has commanded baptism, and lordship demands obedience. If we refuse to obey this simple command, then how in the world could we possibly believe that we will be ready for the more challenging elements of following Jesus?

This is typically one of the first steps of obedience in a Christ-follower's life, but many times it is not taught. People simply do not know that baptism is what God desires. Often days, months, and years can go by before this command is pointed out. Unfortunately, baptism then can become a barrier instead of a blessing. People may want to prove that they are "okay" without it or that it is not "necessary" for salvation. Arguing these points often causes hardened hearts to become harder.

It is essential that we teach the true beauty of baptism. Baptism is a gift from God. God wants us to experience Him completely, with our entire being. We receive His love and grace when the Word or gospel message penetrates our hearts. We also experience God's grace with our minds as they are transformed and renewed. God is not satisfied with that though. He wants us to experience this salvation completely.

That includes experiencing His salvation with our bodies. God gives us baptism so that we can enter into His death, burial, and resurrection with every part of who we are, from our hearts to our minds, from our heads to our toes. It is a complete and total experience that entails a complete and total transformation. We become completely God's...mind, body, and soul.

Why would anyone refuse that?

So love the Lord with all of your heart, soul, mind and strength. Love Him with everything you've got. Hold nothing back. The greatest command is holistic in nature. It leaves no wiggle room.

Jesus wants all of you, and He will not settle for less. Jesus came and gave His life as a ransom to redeem you. Salvation is a free gift from God, but it will cost you everything to receive this gift. You will spend your life on something. Why not spend it on what you were created for? Grace is free, but discipleship will cost you your life.

"Then he said to them all: 'If anyone would come after me, he must deny himself and take up his cross daily and follow me. For whoever wants to save his life will lose it, but whoever loses his life for me will save it.'"
Luke 9:23-24

Praying for One is a way to lay down your life every day. Put your agenda aside to take up the mission of Jesus.

"Yes, Lord, give me One!"

IDENTITY

God is totally self-sufficient and self-sustaining. He needs nothing.

God does not need your sacrifices, time, efforts, or money. In short, God does not need you.

But He wants you.

Want is better than need. God desires you. He created you to be with Him in His eternity. God longs for you so deeply that He sent His Son to die for you. God only requires one thing in exchange…everything.

Now you may be thinking, "Hold up there, mister. I thought God's grace was free."

Yes, grace is free. Grace is the gift of unmerited favor. You cannot earn grace, but grace demands a response.

Salvation changes identity. A saved person experiences metamorphic transformation. The core identity of the person is changed from sinner into saint, from imperfect to perfect. That transformation then radiates outward from the center, and behaviors change to match the new identity.

God wants all of you, not just a piece of you. His love is a consuming fire that will purify every element of your being.

Grace is free, but discipleship will cost you everything. You cannot follow Jesus and hold something back. Your full identity must be surrendered to Him.

Jesus had an encounter with a man who decided that the cost of discipleship was too great. In the story of the Rich Young Ruler, a man of considerable power and wealth approached Jesus and asked what he needed to do to inherit eternal life. Jesus responded by telling him to keep the commandments and the man proudly declared that he had indeed done that.

> *"Jesus looked at him and loved him. 'One thing you lack,' he said. 'Go, sell everything you have and give to the poor, and you will have treasure in heaven. Then come, follow me.'*
> *At this the man's face fell. He went away sad, because he had great wealth."*
>
> **Mark 10:21-22**

The man went away sad, but Jesus did not chase him down to renegotiate. There is no doubt that Jesus truly loved the man and wanted him to be His disciple, but discipleship is costly. It is impossible to follow Jesus while holding onto a former identity. In order to be a new creation, the old most be let go.

God longs for you to come to Him and lay down your life at His feet. You are the one thing God wants. Hold nothing back and give Him everything that you are. Then, and only then, authentic discipleship can transpire in your life.

Your identity is the only thing of eternal value you possess, and it is the only thing that God desires. Give yourself fully to Jesus and spend every moment on earth investing in eternity.

THINK ABOUT IT

1. What do you value the most? What captures your heart and affections? What do you daydream about and hope for?

2. Is there any part of your identity that you hesitate to give to God? Are there parts of your life that are off limits to His lordship?

3. How do you feel about the fact that God wants you?

4. Are you willing to respond daily to His grace? In what ways have you already experienced metamorphic transformation?

PRAY ABOUT IT

Offer yourself fully to God. Give Him every part of your identity. Ask God to make His desires your desires. Pray for One and commit yourself to building His Kingdom today.

NOTES:

KNOW

Do you know Jesus?

Now that is a fantastic question. It is one worthy of deep consideration and honest response.

We live in a culture that has information at our fingertips. We never have to wonder about anything for longer than a few moments because we hold the world in the palm of our hands. A simple Internet search can reveal anything we want to know.

We used to engage in conversations that were full of personal revelations, open-ended questions, and lively debate. Today, most interactions are shut down when someone says, "Hold on…I'll look it up."

Knowledge is a powerful thing, but the readiness of information has added to the growing confusion of knowing versus knowing. It is possible to know all manner of facts about a subject without knowing how to think or apply that information. **Many people know all about Jesus but do not know Jesus.** Relational knowledge is different from factual knowledge. You could read a good biography or even an autobiography about a famous historical figure, but no amount of factual knowledge can add up to knowing the person.

Facts, dates, important events, and amusing anecdotes can certainly enhance relational knowledge, but they can never replace relational knowledge. I have met numerous people over the years that studied Jesus but did not know Him. They knew their facts and could quote the Bible with great intellectual fervor. They were able to pick apart the subtle nuances of scripture and could wax eloquently on a wide range of theological topics. But all of that knowledge was worthless without knowing Jesus.

So, back to the original question…do you know Jesus?

Is He your friend? Is He your master? Is He your Lord? Is He your savior? Who is Jesus to you?

If you fully know Jesus, then your answer is a beautiful mosaic of all types of relational components. A relationship with Jesus is dynamic and progressive in nature. A key phrase that anyone who knows Jesus will arrive at when describing a relationship with Him is "I love Him."

> *"We know that 'We all possess knowledge.' But knowledge puffs up while love builds up. Those who think they know something do not yet know as they ought to know. But whoever loves God is known by God."*
> **1 Corinthians 8:1-3**

God is calling all people into a relationship with Him. He wants us to know Him intimately and eternally. Be certain and secure in your relationship with Jesus. Allow study and biblical knowledge to feed your love for Jesus and guard your heart against substituting information about God for a relationship with God.

Praying for One is a catalyst for knowing the heart of God. When your predominant prayer is a request for God to unleash His love through you, a deeper relational connection is sparked. You begin to want what God wants and love for Him grows.

This simple prayer can drive you into ever-increasing depths of God's love. And whatever knowledge you happen to gain along the way will be put to good use by helping other Ones know Him too.

THINK ABOUT IT

1. Describe the differences between knowing about someone and actually knowing the person relationally.

2. What is required to have a relationship with someone?

3. Have you ever encountered someone who knew about Jesus, but did not know Jesus? Have you ever personally disengaged relationally from Jesus and replaced intimacy with Him with knowledge about Him? Why do you think people do that?

4. How can you know for sure that you are relationally connected to Jesus? What evidence should be present?

PRAY ABOUT IT

Ask God to reveal Himself relationally to you. Seek to know Him and to love Him. Ask God to give you One to share His love with. You cannot share what you do not have, so praying for One opens you up to receive God's love. Know God and make Him known.

NOTES:

CONSUMED

Following Jesus is a consumptive proposition.

Jesus invites us to love Him with every fiber of our beings. We are to love Him with all of our hearts, minds, and bodies. Nothing is held back or placed off-limits. Authentic lordship is all or nothing. We are either all in, or we are not in at all.

Jesus will not be a sometimes Lord, a partial Lord, or a when it's convenient Lord. Jesus is Lord. One day every knee will bow and every tongue will confess that Christ Jesus is Lord. Everything is under His authority, and all will be consumed by His glory.

But is He your Lord?

That is THE question.

Do you know beyond any shadow of a doubt that Jesus is indeed Lord over your life? Have you fully surrendered your identity to Him? Are you consumed heart, mind, and body by Him?

Salvation is a transformational process. We are saved and we are being saved.

Salvation occurs when the core identity is changed from sinner to saint. The Holy Spirit indwells and takes over control. The sinful nature is put to death and rendered powerless. We take on God's identity and then begin the process of living out our new reality. **The change that God originates at the center of our beings radiates outward and consumes every element of identity.**

Jesus was asked what the greatest commandment is and His response was crystal clear.

> "One of the teachers of the law came and heard them debating. Noticing that Jesus had given them a good answer, he asked him, 'Of all the commandments, which is the most important?'
>
> 'The most important one,' answered Jesus, 'is this: "Hear, O Israel: The Lord our God, the Lord is one. Love the Lord your God with all your heart and with all your soul and with all your mind and with all your strength." The second is this: "Love your neighbor as yourself." There is no commandment greater than these.'"

Mark 12:28-31

We are created to love God with everything we've got. Praying for One is a way to do this intentionally and daily.

When we pray for One, we align our hearts with God's heart. We want what He wants. We ask for His perfect love to move through us.

When we pray for One, we fix our minds on God's thoughts. We think with eternity in mind. We see beyond the here and now and are able to process information and prioritize appropriately. We think of ourselves as objects of God's mercy that are redeemed for His purposes.

When we pray for One, we offer our bodies as living sacrifices to God to use as He desires. Our strength, energy, and time are surrendered to God to build His eternal Kingdom.

Pray for One and allow God's love to consume you. The end result will be ultimate soul satisfaction and more people in the Kingdom of Heaven.

THINK ABOUT IT

1. Are you ever tempted to compartmentalize your life with Jesus? Do you give Him full reign in certain areas, but place others off-limits from His Lordship? What are the toughest things in your life to surrender to Jesus?

2. Has God changed you at your core? Has He given you a new identity? How do you know? What evidence do you have? Is there anything hindering the acceptance or living out of a new identity in Jesus?

3. What fears do you have about the consuming nature of lordship?

4. Are there parts of you that you are hesitant to surrender? What troubles you about becoming consumed with living to fulfill Christ's mission?

PRAY ABOUT IT

Identify anything that you have withheld from God and purposefully acknowledge and offer each thing to God. Pray for One with the understanding that God will transform you heart, mind, and actions. Ask God to give you a picture of what being consumed by Him looks like.

NOTES:

RESPOND

Declarations of love demand a response. There is no silence more deafening than in the moment after a bold declaration of love. Will there be reciprocation? Will love be unrequited?

God has declared His love for you.

> *"For God so loved the world that he gave his one and only Son, that whoever believes in him shall not perish but have eternal life."*
>
> **John 3:16**

The cross of Jesus is the most wonderful expression of love the world has ever witnessed. Jesus gave His life in order for you to know and love Him for all eternity. His death, burial, and resurrection are an invitation for you to become united with Him in His mission to redeem the world.

There is a proposal on the table.

Will you accept?

Yes or no?

There is no maybe. Maybe is just an indecisive no. No is your answer until you say yes.

But what does yes entail? When you say yes to Jesus' proposal, what exactly are you agreeing to?

Jesus was crystal clear on this issue. He did not sugarcoat it or leave things open for negotiation. Jesus basically stated that responding to His love requires everything. You cannot respond to His love without offering Him everything that you are.

> *"Then he said to them all: 'Whoever wants to be my disciple must deny themselves and take up their cross daily and follow me. For whoever wants to save their life will lose it, but whoever loses their life for me will save it. What good is it for someone to gain the whole world, and yet lose or forfeit their very self?'"*
>
> **Luke 9:23-25**

It makes no sense to withhold anything from Jesus. There is no gain in this world that compares to the ultimate soul satisfaction of being united with your creator. **God loves you completely and He wants you to respond completely.**

Offer God your mind and allow Him to give you a new worldview as you see everything through the lens of lordship.

Offer God your body as you are immersed in His consuming love and are reborn into new life with Christ.

Offer God your heart as you pray for One and make His ultimate desire your ultimate desire.

Get in rhythm with God's will and do not waste a single second, resource, or bit of energy on fruitless pursuits. God has a mission for you. When you say "yes" to Jesus, He transforms you into a seeking and saving Kingdom- building machine!

THINK ABOUT IT

1. Have you ever been in a moment when love was first declared? Were you the declarer or the recipient? Imagine being in a moment like that right now. What does it feel like? How crucial is a response?

2. In what ways has God declared His love for you? What are some specific examples of His declarations?

3. How have you responded to God's love?

4. Have you given yourself fully to Him? If so, how do you know? If you have not, what is holding you back?

PRAY ABOUT IT

Thank God for declaring His love for you in an undeniable way. Spend some time responding to His love. Offer your life fully to Him and hold nothing back. Pray for One and ask God to make His ultimate desire your ultimate desire.

NOTES:

ONE PRAYER DOES IT ALL

chapter five

ONE PRAYER DOES IT ALL

Discipleship is not a linear process. There have been many great attempts to create forms of systematic discipleship. They provide step-by-step manuals for following Jesus. Do this. Take this class. Then take the next class. Join a group. Participate in an outreach event. Witness to a friend. Practice spiritual disciplines. Read this. Pray that. Now hang your certificate on the wall. And POOF! You are a bona fide follower of Jesus.

Discipleship just doesn't work that way.

Following Jesus is an organic process. It is full of life. Every gut-wrenching stumble in His direction reveals that discipleship is a journey and not a destination. You never arrive at discipleship. It is not something to complete or conquer.

This is a significant problem in churches today. Several generations have graduated from discipleship programs and have sufficiently lost the wonder of following Jesus. They completed the system and came out on the other side of discipleship. Now what?

What happens when you are taught to follow a process instead of Jesus? What do you do when the process ends?

We don't need another system. We don't need more hurdles to clear. We don't need more achievement. We just need Jesus. We are desperate for Jesus. We need His love to flow through us to this broken world and to reflect back to the Father. Nothing less will do.

Followers of Jesus do the three things that are commanded in the Great Commandment and the Great Commission. They love God, love people, and make more disciples.

If you genuinely pray for One, all three of these things will happen. It is impossible to pray earnestly for One and not love God, love people, and reproduce spiritually.

Connect to God

Asking God to give you One person to share His love with connects you to the very heartbeat of Jesus. When we want what Jesus wants, we begin to love Him with unparalleled passion. If you really want your relationship with God to grow, then throw yourself into what He is excited about.

Most of the time we pray to convince God to do our will. We beg and plead for Him to intervene and make everything just the way we want it. In essence, when we pray this way, we are asking God to make us the center of the universe. We want people to serve us, circumstances to favor us, and God to obey us.

114

After all, we are entitled, right? We completed the program. We did the steps. We did our part. Now where is that magically perfect life we were promised? I want my dream life now, and I want it on my terms because I know best!

Ugh. My heart aches. How many prayers have I wasted on me? How many requests had nothing to do with following Jesus? How many have revealed the discipleship lies I so eagerly clung to? My idolatrous prayers of self-promotion left me further from Jesus than I ever imagined possible.

It is impossible to follow Jesus when your primary concern is self. Every form of prosperity preaching is an abomination, but the more subtle versions are the most dangerous.

Sure, we can turn on the television and laugh at ridiculous rants of the phony "give to get" messengers. We spot them and scoff at their unenlightened, Antichrist verbiage. The chuckles turn to irritation as we shake condescending heads in disgust and change the channel.

We change the channel, but the encounter is not over. The message lingers. Our laughter and irritation converge into a sick sense of pride. It is easy to mock the far end of the prosperity spectrum while allowing the same seeds of deception to blossom in our hearts. We compare ourselves to the thieving preachers on TV and in doing so readily accept the more subtle principles of greed, selfishness, and idolatry.

There is a steady line of thinking within mainstream Christianity that promotes the premise that if we are good little boys and girls, then nothing bad will ever happen to us. Following Jesus is taught as a safe way for the entire family to experience prosperity, health, and the American Dream. Discipleship is twisted as the aim is shifted from building God's Kingdom to enhancing each individual's kingdom. When the primary concern is how the individual benefits from following Christ, the ultimate goal of discipleship is utterly lost.

Disciples have a functional goal…to make more disciples.

There is no such thing as discipleship without the end result being more disciples. The "mile wide and inch deep" arguments are ridiculous. Authentic discipleship is always deep and wide. Quality disciples will produce more disciples.

Numbers matter. Reproduction matters. People being saved matters. Jesus didn't die so that His Church could sit around in holy huddles comparing their knowledge of scripture against one another. Jesus didn't die so that His Church could lead comfortable lives based on the notion that God's primary concern is to make us happy. Jesus did not die so that His Church could ignore His chief concern…to seek and save the lost.

Pray for One, and people will be saved. Pray for One, and God will answer. Pray for One, and exponential growth will become reality.

An important way to measure quality is through the increase in quantity. Disciples make more disciples. It is what we do. If we do not make more disciples, then something is tragically wrong.

Seriously, this is just simple logic. If the point of Christianity is only to become more "Jesus-ly" then wouldn't it make way more sense to die now? Let's all just die and appear before Christ at judgment where every impurity will be burned away in an instant. We have been justified through Christ, so let's go ahead and skip out on the painful process of sanctification. What's the point of living and being sanctified if it is not for the mission of Jesus? Christ's Church is here on earth to seek and save the lost.

So do we seek Jesus, grow in our devotion to Him, read the Bible daily, give generously, serve faithfully, participate in small groups, learn, obey, and so on? Of course!

But why?

The foundational reason for doing all the things that we call discipleship is for the purpose of making more disciples. The more we love Jesus, the more we will love His mission. The more we become like Jesus, the more people will be saved because we lay down our lives and take up our crosses to follow Him. The more sacrificial we become, the more we will live to build Christ's eternal Kingdom and the less concern we will have for the temporary things of this world.

Praying for One flips a switch.

It takes the focus off of all things me and puts the focus on all things Jesus. Discipleship is an all Jesus, all the time reality. Praying for One connects us to the heartbeat of Jesus.

Praying for One is a bit painful at first, because you become keenly aware of what you have been praying for. When you begin praying for One, start by taking captive every thought in prayer and make it obedient to Christ. When I did this, I realized that the vast majority of my prayers where about irrelevant things. Praying for personal success, protection, and prosperity was not connecting me to the love of God…it was merely reinforcing my love of self.

I began to replace my prayers for self with prayers for One. I would ramble on honestly about whatever personal concern I had, and then I would say, "But what I really want is One person to share your love with."

The prayers for One steadily became more prevalent as concern for self began to dwindle. The passion that comes from escaping the prison of self and being free to pursue the mission of Christ is impossible to explain. You must experience it for yourself.

Praying for One sets your heart in rhythm with the heartbeat of Jesus. Christianity is a miserable thing indeed when we are out of step with Jesus. There is confusion, doubt, deceit, irritation, conflict, dissension, and the like, when our passion does not match Christ's.

It is impossible to pray earnestly for One and not love God more. When you share His heart, you see even deeper into His love, and that love will explode within you. Our best expression of love to the Father is to do what He commands us to do. Praying for One sets our feet on the path of obedience because concern for self is no longer primary.

Connect to People

So the Great Commandment is to love God with everything you've got, and the second is like it...to love your neighbor as yourself. Do you think that praying for One will help in that whole "loving your neighbor" thing?

When you pray for One, you can't help but love your neighbor. Praying for One establishes you as a love conduit. God's love begins to flow through you to everyone you are connected to. When you make yourself available to God in this fashion, He will place people directly in your path for the purpose of sharing His love.

God's will is that none should perish. God's plan is to use you to extend His grace to others. You are plan A, and there is no plan B. If you refuse to allow God's love to move through you to others, then they will not know the reality of the gospel. Praying for One opens up the floodgates of love and exposes people to the refreshing current of God's mercy.

Praying for One is a perfectly logical way to respond to the salvation and calling of Jesus. Christians are always clamoring on about seeking God's will. The Kingdom of Heaven would be way better off if we stopped asking the same question over and over again and simply accepted the answer God has given. God's will is obvious. Make disciples.

The only way to become confused is to make this complex. We often make this complex to find justification for fruitless living. There is no justification for fruitless living. Either you are making disciples, or you are not. Either you are living for Jesus, or you are not. Either Jesus is Lord, or you are lost.

When you pray for One, God says, "YES!"

This can be the boldest prayer you've ever prayed because it is one that can be expressed with extreme confidence. There is no mystery here. When you ask God to give you One to share His love with, how do you think He will respond?

God's not going to say, "Well, isn't that sweet? I appreciate your willingness to help out, but I've got this one all taken care of. You've done enough already. Heaven's got plenty of people. I don't really care about those who don't know me. We will go ahead and let them experience eternal separation from me. Instead of sharing my love, why don't you just hoard it and allow it to fester in your heart? That way you can be spoiled rotten from the inside out and become repulsive instead of attractive to those who do not know me."

God says yes to our prayers for One because His love must be shared. His love is a fresh commodity. If you hold it in your heart instead of releasing it to others, His love will rot.

There really is nothing more disgusting than a spoiled Christian. When God's love is not released, there is a sickening turn inward. We begin to consider every thought through the filter of self instead of through the mission of Christ. The inward turn plunges us in a downward descent of depravity. It throws the door open for the most dangerous of all sins...self-righteousness.

Praying for One removes the focus from self and places it squarely on building Christ's Kingdom. We are inspired to a noble cause and are able to transcend self in an upward capacity.

Following Jesus is the liberation from self. We escape the torment of being our own god. We become a part of building His eternal Kingdom instead of merely tinkering in our private affairs. Life only makes sense when it is lived in the context of eternity. Eternity only holds hope when it is viewed in the context of Jesus. Jesus only changes us when He is truly Lord. Lordship only occurs through total surrender. Surrender can only happen when we are willing to abandon self.

When pleas for One become your ultimate prayer, you are set free from the bondage of self and can truly love your neighbor. It is fantastic. This is the expressed will of God. He will answer your prayers for One with a resounding, "YES!"

It's kind of like a teenager asking his mom if it would be okay if he cleaned his room. How's mom going to respond to that question? Her initial reaction may be to faint, but after she is revived the answer will be "Yes!" "Yes, son, you may clean your room. What do you need in order to do a good job? Is there a way that I can help you? Thank you for participating in my mission to maintain our home."

God will use you if you let Him. God will transform you if you allow Him. God will love people through you if you are open to Him. The heart change that comes as a result of praying for One radically alters your worldview. People are no longer irritations to be avoided; they are opportunities to be experienced.

God wants people in this world to know how much they are loved, and His Church is the chosen vehicle for delivering His love. God loves people through us, but we must be available, alert, and aggressive with His love. The love of God is not some kind of non-renewable resource that needs to be hoarded in case of shortages.

Love grows as it is shared. The only time that it is in short supply is when it is blockaded within the human heart. Try to hold God's love inside by refusing to share it, and the ceaseless flow is dammed. Open the floodgates by praying for One, and the refreshing flow of God's grace, mercy, and love rushes over the parched and desperate land. The dead are brought to life. The weary are refreshed. His love heals, restores, and revives.

God's love is sufficient, but only if it is shared. People need to be touched by the love of God. The real-world experience of receiving love is not a mystical connection with an undefined source. God puts a face to love by using His people.

Praying for One makes us an extension of God's love. It's kind of like an electrical power strip. We plug into the source by connecting to God and receiving His love. Then we plug into others so that the love of God is channeled through us to them. Then they plug into others and to others and to others until the whole world is connected to the eternal source of authentic love.

When you pray for One, a switch gets flipped in your heart. There is a change in purpose. You begin to look at people differently. There is an expectation that every encounter is an opportunity for God's love to be experienced through you. In the middle of casual conversations, you will be struck by the reality that "this could be my One."

You will find yourself praying ceaselessly in the midst of everyday life for wisdom, courage, and compassion. People will see something different in you, and they will expose themselves in surprising ways. You will be in over your head. Human wisdom will not suffice. You will be forced to depend on the power of the Holy Spirit dwelling within you. It can be a terrifying thing, but when you yield to God's love, His truth will rush out of you and wash over others.

Praying for One moves us beyond the placating lies of our cultural norms and into the raw and authentic truth. When you pray for One, loving truth begins to pour out of you into others. The authenticity of God's love is thoroughly disarming. People are so used to being lied to that when they hear loving truth, they stop dead in their tracks.

I once encountered a man after one of our worship services who was visibly shaken by what he had just experienced. He came out of the auditorium before the service was over. The lobby was fairly empty, and I was sitting on a stool off to the side. As he got closer to me, I could see the mixture of emotion in his face. There was fear, anger, doubt, despair, grief, and guilt. The flood of emotion was more than he could handle, and tears began to stream down his weathered cheeks.

I leaned forward and made eye contact with him. I asked if he was okay, and he responded, "No." I asked what was going on, and he told me that he had never experienced anything like our church. He said that the presence of God was undeniable, and he knew that he needed God's love, but he said he couldn't stay. When I asked why he couldn't stay, his voice faltered and cracked as he barely breathed the words, "I'm not worthy."

My initial reaction was to say, "Yes, you are. You are worthy. Don't leave." I opened my mouth, but the look on his face was too real for me to spin some kind of condescending lie. He knew he was not worthy, and so did I.

The look on my face was sufficient truth for him, and he gave a simple nod and began to walk away. In my spirit, I was crying out to God. In that instant, I loved this man in a way that I will never be able to explain. I prayed, "Help me God," as I watched the man walking away.

Then without thinking, I stood and yelled, "STOP!" Everyone in the lobby froze. The man turned and looked at me. He was defeated and done, but there was a flicker of hope deep within his eyes. This was a holy moment.

I pointed at him and excitedly said, "Neither am I."

Those words of simple truth hit him like a surge of electricity. His countenance changed, and he moved toward me. I put my hand on his shoulder, and I told him the truth, "I'm not worthy either. None of us are. We all need grace."

Praying for One frees you to love people with truth. The awareness that comes from expecting God to answer your most passionate plea sets your mind ready for action. In the moment of truth...when your One is standing before you...your soul will leap with anticipation over what God is about to do.

His love is contagious. It spreads like wildfire. God's love moves through a gentle touch, an encouraging word, an act of kindness, a generous gesture, and the like. God works through the simple and uses the available. That's the beauty of praying for One. Simply put, it makes you available.

Connect to Mission

Every person you encounter is a potential One. Every appointment is divine. Every conversation is a unique opportunity to share God's love. Every day has a purpose, and each moment is filled with mission.

When you awake each morning with a prayer for One on your lips, there is no confusion about what the day will hold. The gospel is each day's destination. It doesn't matter where you go or what you do...the end result is still the same...people are going to be saved!

Please understand this. If you pray for One, people will be saved. God will use you. He will say "Yes" to your predominant prayer.

God will use YOU. The prevailing attitude is that God only uses pastors and religious leaders for this sort of thing, but the truth of the matter is that pastors are the most likely to mess this up. We complicate things. We overthink things. We rationalize and justify. We philosophize and theorize. We get hung up on theological concepts and question everything. We get paralyzed in the minutia.

Just pray for One, and then get your head out of the sand. That's our biggest problem on the missional front...we bury our heads in the sand and pretend that the lost are not a reality. One of the greatest barriers to evangelism is that many Christians will claim that they do not know any lost people. I'm not buying that, and neither should you.

Pull your head out, and take a look around. Pray for One, and God will place people directly in your path. Lost people are everywhere. They live in your neighborhood, work in your office, exercise at your gym, wait on your table, teach your kids, pick up your trash, deliver your mail, treat your illnesses, and so on.

The problem with our thinking is the word "your" in the previous sentence. We tend to view people as being in our world, on our turf, for the purpose of meeting our needs. If you are a Christian, this is not your world. You are a stranger and an alien here. You have a heavenly home. Our time on this planet is to be spent intentionally serving as ambassadors for our eternal home.

Egocentrism places self at the center of an individual's universe and assumes that everything else will revolve around and support the all-important core. All emphasis is placed on "me" as life is carried out in a series of self-serving events. This inward focus slams tight the door to the prison of self and intense sadness consumes the inmate. Desperate longing ensues as no satisfaction can be found. We are compelled to transcend self, but we do not know how.

Initial attempts to escape the prison of self are often spent in humanitarian efforts. This parallel transcendence of self produces momentary feelings of satisfaction as we seek to meet the needs of others. Our "good deeds" feel good indeed, but they are not good enough.

It doesn't take long to realize that the needs are greater than we can meet. With every act of kindness comes the recognition that our human efforts are insufficient. We cannot do enough. We serve one, and there are one hundred more whose needs go unmet. The unfairness of life overwhelms. Our good deeds are met with resistance, and positive efforts can even produce negative results. Those we help take advantage of us, turn on us, reject us, and punish us.

Frustration sets in and drives us deeper into the depths of self with even more intense feelings of sadness and hopelessness. We lose faith in our fellow humans and rightly so. People disappoint because they are flawed. They are not worthy of our faith any more than we are worthy of theirs. Humanitarian efforts without divine intervention do nothing for the long-term escape from self.

I certainly am not proposing that we not serve others. The point is that serving others is only effective in the long run if it points both the server and the one being served toward relationship with Jesus. Self-generated efforts always lead to a deeper turn inwards.

Another way that we attempt to escape self is through downward transcendence. Most often this is expressed through self-destructive behaviors. Addiction, abuse, and indulgence in sin create a temporary euphoria, but the momentary escape carries a hefty price. Guilt, shame, paranoia, and the fixation with finding the next fix overwhelm.

Attempts to escape self through descending behaviors will ultimately result in destruction. Pleasure seeking outside of a relationship with Jesus plunges us into a type of solitary confinement. This adds loneliness to the previously mentioned sadness and hopelessness.

Parallel and downward transcendence of self only serve to make matters worse, but there is another option. We can transcend self upwardly through a relationship with God. When this occurs, every notion of self is replaced with Lordship. God provides purpose, meaning, hope, happiness, satisfaction, pleasure, and all things good.

God uses us to serve others, but our efforts always point to Him. This mitigates the problems with parallel transcendence because God is capable of meeting all needs. We are not overwhelmed with the unfairness of this world because our focus is out of this world. People can still reject, abuse, and punish us, but what does that matter? We are no longer our own. We serve another. Self no longer has power to control, so things that would have previously impacted us negatively are rendered impotent.

Upward transcendence opens the door for ultimate soul satisfaction. We are free to experience pleasure through relationship with Jesus. Be warned…addiction is a virtual guarantee, but it is the best kind of addiction. When you pray for One, intense pleasure is experienced every time God provides another to share His love with. I have never met anyone who prayed for One, got One, and then thought that One was enough.

One is never enough! Praying for One is addictive in the purest sense. It will take over every aspect of your life as you are consumed with the mission of Jesus to seek and save the lost. Upward transcendence through praying for One destroys sadness, hopelessness, and loneliness because we are consumed with building into God's eternal Kingdom. This is the only valid escape from the prison of self.

The Great Commandment of loving God and loving others provides the fuel for living out the Great Commission of making disciples. When you love God, you must love others because you are connected to the source of love, and it must flow through you. When you love others, you must share Jesus with them because love requires action.

Love is not passive. It is not passive-aggressive. It is aggressive-aggressive.

Authentic followers of Christ are compelled to action. They are sucked into the divine fray. It is impossible to be a passive spectator in the Kingdom-building work of Jesus. When you belong to Him, you become much more than a recipient of grace… you become a participant in grace.

127

Others will experience God's eternal power and divine nature through you as Jesus makes Himself known in you. Christ's Church is His physical presence on earth, and He makes His appeal through us. He reconciles humankind to Himself, and Christians are entrusted with the ministry of reconciliation.

We are God's plan A, and there is no plan B.

When we refuse to participate in His mission, people are not saved. There is gravity to this gut-wrenching truth that must capture our attention and move us to drastic action. We are responsible.

Yes...Jesus does the redemptive work, but we share in this work. We know that salvation can only come through Jesus, but the message must come through His Body. Jesus took sin inside of Himself, put it to death on the cross, and conquered death through His resurrection. Sin remained dead, but He is alive. Eternal life is found only through sharing in His resurrection.

We are created in God's image for the purpose of partnership. The first command God gave Adam and Eve was to be fruitful and multiply. That same command applies today. We must be fruitful and multiply. Praying for One sets our course in this direction and maintains consistent and steady aim.

How do we know if we are successful in life? We are only successful if the Creator's purpose is fulfilled in us. His purpose is for us to partner with Him in His work. Are more people in the Kingdom of Heaven because of how God uses you? This really is the only question that matters.

Pray for One, and your aim will be right. You can't hit what you don't aim for. People do not just accidentally fall into discipleship. Discipleship occurs through concerted effort and prayerful devotion.

Disciples do what Jesus did. What did Jesus do? He made disciples. Disciples make disciples. Period.

If you are not reproducing spiritually, then you are not a disciple of Jesus. There is no way around this simple logic. The plain truth is before us. How will we respond?

My response is to pray for One because when I pray for One, people are saved. I love God more. I love people more. I love Christ's mission more. One prayer does it all.

CONNECT

The fundamental disconnect within much of Christianity is that those who claim to be disciples of Jesus are not actually producing the fruit that Jesus produced.

Jesus made disciples. It is what He did. If we follow Jesus and do what He did, then we will make more disciples.

The logic is simple, but the excuses abound. People often defend their lack of production with pharisaical zeal.

Why defend that?

We ought to be grieved over the masses of people who do not yet know Jesus. We ought to be broken-hearted and compelled to take action. We ought to never waste a single ounce of energy on foolish excuses while the lost are still hopelessly adrift upon the sea of sin.

God took drastic action, and if we are truly His followers, so will we. When we connect with God, His desire moves through us and becomes our dominant desire. We become consumed with what consumes Him, and we will not stop until every One is found.

In John 15, Jesus speaks about the critical nature of bearing fruit. **Reproducing spiritually is not optional. If we are deeply connected to Christ, it is inevitable.** If we remain connected to Him, we will bear fruit. Nonproducing branches are removed because they hinder the vine's ability to grow.

"I am the true vine, and my Father is the gardener. He cuts off every branch in me that bears no fruit, while every branch that does bear fruit he prunes so that it will be even more

fruitful. You are already clean because of the word I have spoken to you. Remain in me, as I also remain in you. No branch can bear fruit by itself; it must remain in the vine. Neither can you bear fruit unless you remain in me.

"I am the vine; you are the branches. If you remain in me and I in you, you will bear much fruit; apart from me you can do nothing."

John 15:1-5

Praying for One is a practical way to connect daily to the heartbeat of God. When your dominant prayer is laced with the desire to seek and save the lost, your connection to God becomes paramount. It is impossible to bear fruit apart from Him, and it is impossible not to bear fruit when connected to Him.

Examine your life. Are you fully connected to God? If you are unsure, ask God to show you. Ask Him how He is using you to help others connect to Him.

Christians are to be the light of the world, but a light is useless if it is not plugged into the power source. Our first priority every day is to connect to God in prayer. Before doing anything else, we must humbly seek Him and exalt Him as Lord. As we do this, we position ourselves to be used by God. An expectation arises that the day will not be wasted. Hope springs forth that God will use us as a part of His divine plan to save the world. His desire begins to pulsate through us, and we are prepared and compelled to take action.

Aligning your will to God's will in prayer is critical. We will never experience the abundant life that Jesus promises without first having the desire to do His will. Without this critical connection, we will have the wrong expectations and will experience perpetual disappointment. But when the connection is present, we will want what God wants and this never disappoints.

THINK ABOUT IT

1. What do you pray about the most?

2. Do you feel connected to God through prayer? Why or why not?

3. Is God using you to make more disciples? If so, how? If not, why not?

4. What did Jesus promise would be the end result of remaining in Him? Is it possible to produce any eternal fruit apart from Him? What is your life producing now?

PRAY ABOUT IT

Intentionally connect to God. Exalt His desires over your own. Ask Him what He wants and then ask Him to change your heart. Pray for One and set the proper expectation for your day.

NOTES:

GOD

The accepted line of thinking goes something like this: "If I behave myself and act like a good person, then nothing bad will happen to me."

How is that working out for you?

When Christianity becomes about pain avoidance there is zero hope of actually being able to follow Jesus. Pain avoidance puts the focus on me. If my prayers are primarily about my comfort, success, welfare, and so on then who should I assume is my lord? Jesus is not Lord when your primary concern is not to honor and obey Him.

Lordship is a daily issue for those who claim to know Jesus. We must die to self daily by laying down our lives and taking up crosses to follow Him. It is absurd to think that because that decision was made at some point in the past that we do not need to make it again each day. It is impossible to follow Jesus without purposefully setting Him apart as Lord in your heart each day. Failing to do this results in reverting to primal instincts of self-preservation.

That is simply the natural order of things, but God is calling us to be a part of the supernatural. By connecting with God, we have the opportunity to transcend self to become participants in building His eternal Kingdom. A true connection with God always puts self on the backburner. We are no longer first. In fact, we are not even second. Authentic lordship ensures a third place finish at best.

God is first. His mission is primary. Any exaltation of self over Him blocks that connection. People are second. You cannot expect to follow Jesus without putting the needs of others above your own. Sacrifice is normative. **Why would Jesus tell us to take up crosses if He did not intend for us to use them?** Our surprise and anger regarding personal sacrifice reveals fatal lordship issues.

Praying for One sets the mind on what God desires and prepares us for action. It is a classic "thy will be done" prayer. We ask God to use us even though we know it is going to involve sacrifice and suffering because our primary concern is to do His will.

When Jesus prayed in the garden of Gethsemane on the night of His betrayal, it was not the first time that His life was in jeopardy. There had been several other attempts on His life, but it had not been His time. In one occurrence Jesus simply walked through an angry mob and they did not touch Him. At other times, the scriptures simply say that He slipped away. That night in the garden would be different. His time had come, so He prayed.

"Father, if you are willing, take this cup from me; yet not my will, but yours be done." An angel from heaven appeared to him and strengthened him. And being in anguish, he prayed more earnestly, and his sweat was like drops of blood falling to the ground.

Luke 22:42-44

Our God understands our struggle to put His will first. He is gracious and compassionate as He allows us to meet with Him in prayer to firmly establish whose will wins out. Real connections with God take us to the place of relinquishing our wills to His. Prayer is no longer about attempts to manipulate God to do our will, but is about being aligned with His will.

Praying for One facilitates this connection by making our

primary prayer concern an issue of His mission to save the world. "God, use me," allows for a much stronger connection than "God, bless me."

If you are connected to God, you already are blessed. If you are saved, you are blessed. Christians do not seek God's blessing, we are God's blessing. Connect to Him and He will bless others through you.

THINK ABOUT IT

1. Have you ever been frustrated with God because of some difficulty you were facing? What produced the frustration? How did you deal with it? How did it impact your relationship with God?

2. What do you think Jesus meant when He said that in order to follow Him we must take up our crosses? What are some ways that you can sacrifice so others can know Him?

3. What do you think it means to be blessed by God?

4. Are you blessed? Does your relationship with Him ensure eternal blessings for you? What is the best thing you could do with God's blessings?

PRAY ABOUT IT

Echo the words of Jesus in prayer by saying to God, "Not my will but yours be done." Connect with God by acknowledging that you are indeed blessed and then ask Him to use you to bless others. Pray for One.

NOTES:

PEOPLE

People need people.

We are created with deep relational needs, but sin destroys relational intimacy. Loneliness is a condition that plagues humanity. Even people who have a high degree of social interaction struggle with loneliness. Most people deeply fear baring their souls to one another.

The fear is real and justified. We know that people are judging us because we judge others. We assign value to people based on what we believe they can do for us. When others fail to meet our expectations, we devalue them and at a certain point, determine that the relationship has a negative value.

Trying to connect with people is impossible with this type of worldview. People will always let you down because all people are flawed. They can never measure up, and relationships remain in a perpetual state of brokenness due to faulty expectations.

But what if we looked at people differently?

What if we assigned value based on God's love for each person? What if we saw others as objects of God's love, and we viewed ourselves as the distributors? Relational connectivity could flourish in that kind of environment.

Praying for One lays the groundwork for this shift in thinking to occur. Anyone could be your One. **When your only expectation for another human is for them to be an object of love, the relationship dynamic changes dynamically.**

Jesus gave us a new command. He told us to love one another. This is our paramount responsibility when it comes to relationships and it is a game changer.

"A new command I give you: Love one another. As I have loved you, so you must love one another. By this everyone will know that you are my disciples, if you love one another."
John 13:34-35

When your primary purpose for relationships is to love like Jesus loves, you are set free from the broken pattern of this world. You allow yourself to love others selflessly. The return on your love investment is not reciprocated love, but joy and satisfaction from allowing God's love to move through you.

This critical shift in relational thinking becomes the driving force for healing, restoration, and sustainability. Consider how families could be transformed if even just one member would love like this. Authentic, Christ-centered love is compelling and contagious. People long to love like this but do not know how. It is so radically different from everything we have experienced and learned.

Praying for One sets a course for new behaviors. When you view people (even difficult people) as answers to prayer, you stop expecting them to do anything for you because by existing they have done enough. Their mere presence is sufficient because your primary desire is to allow God to love on them through you. There is no personal offense if God's love is rejected. There may be sadness and disappointment, but love does not cease. You are free to sacrificially extend yourself as an agent of God's love without worrying about a broken heart.

This is not wishful thinking. This is truth. God wants to use you to love people. Ask Him to give you One, and your eyes will be opened to see as He sees. EveryOne has value. For God so loved the world that He gave His one and only Son. Will you allow God to give His Son's love through you?

THINK ABOUT IT

1. What relational fears do you have?

2. What are three ways you typically assign value to others?

3. Think about a broken relationship you have experienced. What harmed the relationship? What factors led to the relationship's demise?

4. How have your expectations negatively impacted your ability to relate to other people?

PRAY ABOUT IT

Ask God to show you how you have contributed to relational brokenness. Offer yourself fully to God as a dispenser of His love. Pray for One and ask God to help you look at everyOne like He does.

NOTES:

MISSION

Life with Jesus cannot make sense when His mission is not our primary objective. This is the grand frustration that plagues everyone who accepts salvation but rejects the new identity and purpose that comes from being united with Christ.

The joy of salvation fades as the process of stumbling after Jesus proves to be more arduous than we ever anticipated. We begin to question the commands of Christ. We wonder if the sacrifice required to follow Him is worth it. We start to think that we could be happier if we did things our own way.

In some regards, we are correct. If we are not consumed with seeking and saving the lost, then actually following Jesus will produce little to no satisfaction. Without a dramatic shift in missional philosophy we are left to assume that being a Christian will make us healthy, wealthy, and wise. It is impossible to deal with frustration and difficulties when the primary motivation is wrong.

Me-centered Christianity cannot work. It is a lie that deludes the mind and dilutes the power and purpose of the Church. **Following hard after Jesus is never primarily about me becoming a better me. It is about being used by Him to do what He came to do.**

We are resources that Jesus purchased through His death on the cross. We belong to Him to be used for His purpose. We are reborn into an eternal Kingdom and are deployed by Jesus to do His will.

I have heard it argued that the primary purpose of Christians is to glorify God. I will not debate that premise, but I will point out the abstract nature at its core. Glorifying God is great, but how do you do that? How does that abstract become tangible? What evidence can we expect to know that God is indeed being glorified?

God's glory resounds. It echoes and grows. When He is glorified in us through obedient, purposeful lives, reproduction will occur. Praying for One sets a glorification expectation. When we constantly ask God to use us to share His love with others, we become obsessed with His good, pleasing, and perfect will. Following Jesus makes sense because it is no longer abstract. Ones are being saved. Obedience and sacrifice add up to something of eternal value.

Praying for One is a daily reminder of who we are in Christ Jesus and of the mission He calls us to.

"For we are God's handiwork, created in Christ Jesus to do good works, which God prepared in advance for us to do."
Ephesians 2:10

The rebirth of a Christian brings a transformation in purpose. There are good works that God has prepared for us to do. Failure to obey brings catastrophic consequences. It is tempting to rationalize that our disobedience only harms us, but that is ultimate foolishness. If you were to flip that argument then you would assume that obedience only blesses us.

We are not who are at stake. If you are saved, then hallelujah… thank you, Jesus! Salvation is by grace through faith and not by works so no one can boast. Jesus saved us for His sake, and following Him is all about fulfilling His mission. The true joy of salvation can only be realized through connecting with the mission of Jesus to seek and save the lost.

THINK ABOUT IT

1. What are some ways that you can glorify God?

2. What could following Jesus cost you? Make a list of five specific things.

3. Is obedience to Jesus worth the cost? Why or why not?

4. What should you expect the blessing of obedience to be?

PRAY ABOUT IT

Thank God for saving you. Spend a few moments reflecting on how great His salvation is. Commit to sharing His salvation with others. Pray for One and remember that you are God's handiwork.

NOTES:

CHURCH IN 3D

chapter six

CHURCH IN 3D

One of the greatest issues that many Christians run into is that our faith is flat. It sounds like Christianity. It bears a resemblance to Christianity. But there is no depth. Something is missing.

We tend to resemble the churches we attend, and in the last couple of decades, there has been movement in many churches to become one-dimensional. They emphasize one primary category while de-emphasizing others. The church and its members define themselves and express their faith in Jesus in a one-dimensional fashion.

God is a three-dimensional God. He is the Father, Son, and Holy Spirit. We are made in His image. We are three-dimensional people. We are soul, mind, and body. A relationship between a three-dimensional God and three-dimensional people should be experienced in a three-dimensional fashion.

So, what we need are three-dimensional churches that love

God, love people, and love the mission of Jesus. We need churches that do things like pray for One because praying for One opens up a community of believers to the fullness of discipleship.

It is similar to the age-old argument that churches have had for years. "Are we going to be a church that disciples or a church that evangelizes?" YES!

You cannot be one without being the other. Discipleship and evangelism always go hand-in-hand. It is impossible to separate the two. If people are growing in their love for God and love for people, then they will reproduce spiritually. Separating discipleship from evangelism is insane, but what is even crazier is the tendency to pit them against each other like they are in competition with one another.

Church leaders struggle with how to allocate limited resources and feel forced to choose between inward- and outward-focused programs. Tension arises between meeting needs within the body and reaching out into the community. Praying for One breaks this tension by keeping our aim always on the functional purpose of the Church. There is no distinction between outreach and in-reach because everything is done for the purpose of seeing more people in the Kingdom of Heaven.

Do we provide pastoral care? Yes, because it helps get more people into the Kingdom of Heaven. Do we do children's programs? Yes, because they help get more people into the Kingdom of Heaven. Do we have small groups, take mission trips, and have killer weekend worship services? Yes, because they help get more people into the Kingdom of Heaven.

In recent years certain buzzwords have emerged to describe three primary types of churches. There are attractional, relational, and missional churches. Each type of church will tell you that their methodology is the right way of doing things and can point out the shortcomings of the others. The problem is that they are all one-dimensional and lacking what the others offer. All three models have value, but their true worth can only be experienced when they are expressed in concert with one another.

connecting people to God

Attractional churches place their focus on connecting people to God. The weekend worship services are often the defining element of the church as people are invited to come and see how great God is. The love of Jesus is experienced through presentation that is well prepared, intentional, engaging, entertaining, compelling, culturally relevant, and full of excellence. High emphasis is placed on members inviting people to church.

Attractional churches pay close attention to what people will experience when they attend a worship service. Buildings are designed to be inviting, comfortable, clean, and easy to navigate. Greeters are often stationed in the parking lot to create a welcoming feeling. Children's ministries are presented as safe, fun, and appealing. The church is sensitive to guests and makes great efforts to attract, welcome, and retain new people.

connecting people to people

Relational churches place their focus on connecting people to people. Community is the defining element of the church as people are encouraged to express the love of God through relational experiences. Small groups are key.

These churches vary in size from individual house churches to huge mega churches, but conceptually they share the same driving force. Everything revolves around relational connectivity. Emphasis is placed on mentoring, personal discipleship, discussion, and intimacy. The church is often decentralized, as the focus is less on a church building and more home-based.

A great deal of effort is placed into the development and promotion of a dynamic network of groups that collectively represent the mission of the church. People are often invited into a small group experience before they ever attend a larger worship gathering. Relational churches recognize that the first and greatest human problem is loneliness, and they make attacking loneliness their number one priority.

connecting people to mission

Missional churches place their focus on connecting people to mission. Active expressions of faith in Jesus are what define the church, and people are encouraged to live out their faith in the real world. Community service, generosity, and meeting physical needs are primary ways that the gospel is shared with others.

Missional churches are less "come and see" and more "go and do" in their methodology. Emphasis is moved away from anything deemed inward-focused and placed on sending Christians out. It is not uncommon for missional churches to cancel weekend services on occasion to utilize that time to be involved in some form of community action. Members see themselves as an integral part of the mission of the church because participation in the church is centered around active expressions of faith.

Each of these dimensions holds extreme value, but if one is highlighted disproportionately over the others, problems will ensue.

Attractional churches often become more about the show than the gospel. When the emphasis is all on attracting people, the desire not to offend can strip the gospel of power. Pride enters through the competitive nature of comparing numbers. There can be a "my church is better than your church because we have more people in our services" mentality. A revolving door effect begins as people are drawn in for a period of time and then exit because they desire more. The show is not sufficient. People in attractional churches often feel disconnected from others and struggle to find outlets to appropriately express their faith in Jesus.

Relational churches often struggle with legalism, cliquishness, and low evangelistic energy. When the emphasis is all on connecting relationally with other Christians, the "holy huddle" effect takes hold. The church has a tendency to turn inward, latch on to one another, and guard against evil outside influences. Pride enters through comparing relative holiness. There can be a "my church is better than your church because we have more spiritual depth" mentality. People in relational churches can struggle to see the connection between their faith experience and the overall mission of Christ to seek and save the lost.

Missional churches often become so action-oriented that they forget the crucial nature of words and worship. The gospel must be preached with words. How can people hear if the gospel is not preached? God is also revealed through the worship of His people. Allowing people who are apart from Christ to experience authentic worship is one of the best ways to demonstrate the reality of a God who loves them. When the emphasis is all on going and doing, one of the best evangelistic tools the church has to offer is neglected as the corporate worship gathering is relegated to a second- or third-tier experience. Things as simple as cancelling a Sunday morning worship service to go and serve the community can communicate to the church that worshiping together in the classic sense does not hold much value. Pride enters through becoming works-based instead of faith-based. There can be a "my church is better than your church because we do more for the community" mentality. People in missional churches can lose sight of the awesomeness of communal worship and the critical component of preaching the gospel with words.

The Body of Christ is attractional, relational, and missional. It is all three and should never be experienced without the depth that the three-in-one provide. A one-dimensional church is out of balance and off kilter. It doesn't take long for it to start missing the mark. The functional aim will move away from more people in the Kingdom of Heaven and become about something else. A minor deviation in aim, experienced over time, will cause the Church to become utterly ineffective in seeking and saving the lost.

aim over time

The more time that passes, the greater the chance of missing the mark.

The tension between the three dimensions is critical to keep the Church on point. Praying for One creates a church environment that is attractional, relational, and missional. When the primary prayer on every member's lips is for God to give them each One person to share His love with, there is an explosion of depth and fruitfulness.

The aim of the Church is correct because everyone wants the same thing…more people in the Kingdom of Heaven. There is no time or energy for silly arguments about minor doctrines. There is no time or energy for complaining about not being fed. There is no time or energy for dividing over worship styles, building décor, small group methodology, personal offenses, and the like.

When the thrust of the Church is praying for One, it is propelled into exponential multiplication. The force of this movement is so great that everyone hangs on for the ride of their lives. Nobody wants to stop praying for One because life finally makes sense when lived through the mission of Jesus. Since nobody is willing to stop praying for One, the Church must stay on point through being three-dimensional.

Attractional, relational, and missional methodology hold

extreme value when they work in concert with one another. They actually feed into one another and create a cyclical pattern of dynamic growth. These three dimensions are pulled right out of the Great Commandment (to love God and people) and the Great Commission (to make disciples). Praying for One is a thread running through them that binds them together. A church that prays for One can experience the tremendous joy and confidence that comes from being three-dimensional.

The issue surrounding being three-dimensional is not one of balance but one of value. Every church, and every person for that matter, is going to be drawn more heavily to one of the three. They will connect with one more than the others and will highlight that particular dimension. Churches, just like people, have different personalities, and that is part of the beauty of the local church. Praying for One holds the Church accountable to the fullness of discipleship by placing equal value on each dimension. When everyone is praying for One, nobody is willing to settle for less than God's best. We become mature and complete, not lacking anything needed for effective ministry.

Each church will experience varying degrees of effectiveness in each of the three dimensions based on the personality, passions, and resources available to that local congregation. For instance, a church with an amazing building in an excellent location might be more attractional than a church plant meeting in an elementary school buried deep within a neighborhood. It makes sense for each church to emphasize what they are best equipped to do, but at the same time, the depth of all three dimensions must be present.

So, should churches be attractional? Absolutely! Jesus is attractive. The gospel is attractive. Eternal life is attractive. Churches that intentionally sabotage the attractiveness of the gospel would serve Christ's Kingdom better by shutting their doors and never claiming to be a church again. Attractional methodology does not need to be the primary emphasis of every church, but every church should value it. Whatever resources are available should be utilized with excellence. Excellence is not a comparison game because excellence is doing your best with what you have to work with. When you pray for One, there is a desire to invite people to experience the power of God's presence.

Should churches be relational? Of course! Relational connectivity is a crucial component of praying for One. The personal nature of praying for One will drive people into more intimate community. When you pray for One, God increases your relational desires. There is a compulsion to connect with people because every person could be your One. Christ-centered, relational connectivity sends an incredible message to the world. It says, "Look. This is different. Loneliness is not accepted here. We love one another, and you are loved too."

Should churches be missional? Indeed! Authentic faith demands action. Praying for One is certainly not passive. When you pray for One, tangible expressions of faith are required. You go and do so that you can invite people to come and see. God uses His Church in action to put His love on display. It is similar to the miracles. Why did Jesus perform miracles? Scholars and theologians list many reasons, but one of the most compelling is that Jesus is compassionate. His compassionate love moved Him to act. When we pray for One, we tap into the compassionate love of Jesus, and we must release that love into the world around us.

So, what do we conclude? The Church (collectively – all Christians everywhere, locally – groups of Christ followers worshiping together under the authority of a local church, and individually – the personal responsibility to participate in the Great Commandment and Great Commission) must be attractional, relational, and missional. Different elements may be emphasized at times based on a variety of factors, but all must be valued and expressed.

When Christians are flat, they are ineffective. Praying for One provides the necessary depth and preparedness for every good work. Church in 3D is exactly what we need to be. Attractional, relational, and missional methodology working together allow the Church to go all in on building Christ's Kingdom. Pray for One, and you will become attractional, relational, missional, and, most importantly, efficiently effective.

ATTRACTIONAL

God is attractive.

Humans are drawn to their maker. We long to connect to God and to be in His presence. God is love. His very nature is the ultimate thing we all desire. He beckons all people to come to Him to find purpose and true life.

Grace is attractive.

The forgiveness of sin and the redemption provided through Jesus' substitutionary death on the cross compel people to surrender. The promises of rest and reconciliation draw us into Christ's eternal Kingdom. His salvation is beautiful, and His unmerited favor resonates deep within all who understand the nature of their own depravity.

Worship is attractive.

Recognizing the presence of God and responding appropriately by exalting Him are exhilarating. In meaningful moments of worship, time stands still because we are experiencing the eternal nature of God's presence. Worship is a little glimpse of heaven on earth. God is revealed through the worship of His people.

The Church is attractive.

The Church is Christ's body and physical presence on earth. There is nothing in this world like the Church. The local church is powerful and has authority in the name of Jesus to do mighty things. Jesus uses His Church to make His appeal to all those who are separated from Him. People long to belong, and the Church is where our common identity in Christ can be expressed in victory and freedom.

Are you attractive?

If you are a Christian, you need to understand how important that question is. Eternity is at stake. God is making His appeal through you! **It is crucial that Christ followers allow God to strip away all of our ugliness and shame so that Jesus can be revealed through us.**

> *"We are therefore Christ's ambassadors, as though God were making his appeal through us. We implore you on Christ's behalf: Be reconciled to God."*
>
> **2 Corinthians 5:20**

Think about some of the unattractive character traits that often plague Christians. Things like hatred, bitterness, fear, legalism, self-righteousness, pride, and being judgmental are essentially grace-repellent. When we allow these things to continue in ourselves, we become unattractive. When the Church is unattractive, God is unattractive. We cannot allow this.

The church is designed by God to grow, and it actually takes work to make it unattractive. When we pray for One and understand that each day's destination is the gospel message, we allow God to make us beautiful. The world will be in awe of the beauty of Christ that is revealed in you if you allow Jesus to use you for His glory.

> *"And how can anyone preach unless they are sent? As it is written: 'How beautiful are the feet of those who bring good news!'"*
>
> **Romans 10:15**

We have the best news the world will ever hear. I can think of nothing more attractive than telling the story of Jesus and His salvation. Pray for One. Ask God to give you One today to share His love with. Ask God to remove all ugliness from your character so that Jesus can be seen in you.

THINK ABOUT IT

1. What do you think would compel a church to be intentionally unattractive?

2. What are some ways that churches could be more attractive?

3. What are some things in you that need to change so that Jesus can be seen more clearly through you?

4. Make a list of all the attractive qualities you see in God. Highlight the qualities you see Him producing in you. Circle the ones that you see lacking in your life.

PRAY ABOUT IT

Thank God that He attracted you to Himself. Praise Him for His grace and salvation. Ask Him to make you salt and light in this world. Pray for One and ask God how you can be more attractive to those who are far from Him.

NOTES:

RELATIONAL

God is relational.

He is all about relationships. God's primary concern is for every person to be in an eternal relationship with Him. Jesus came to restore the broken relationship between humankind and our creator.

Consider the effort that God puts into relationships. He holds nothing back as He goes to extravagant measures to engage all people relationally. God's relational desire for us is so great that He gave His one and only Son as a sacrifice to create a way for us to be with Him.

Our relational God is now being revealed to the world through His Church. We must prioritize relationships and realize that they have great purpose and value. Healthy, dynamic relationships reveal God's love to the world.

> *"But in fact God has placed the parts in the body, every one of them, just as he wanted them to be. If they were all one part, where would the body be? As it is, there are many parts, but one body. The eye cannot say to the hand, 'I don't need you!' And the head cannot say to the feet, 'I don't need you!'"*
> **1 Corinthians 12:18-21**

I have known people who disengaged from the church because they thought that they did not need the church. First of all, they were wrong. We all need the church. Secondly, even if they did not need the church, the church needed them. God reveals Himself through His Church, and we need the full body to fully represent God's love.

I think that churches have made mistakes in the ways we promote relational connectivity. When launching small groups or encouraging people to build relationships within the church, the promotional focus is almost exclusively on how being in a group will help the individual grow spiritually. That is a recipe for disaster! If you enter a group with that expectation, you are sure to be disappointed.

The primary purpose of our relationships is not to have our needs met but to share God's love with one another. There is no disappointment in that. You can be in any group and purposefully share God's love. God will be honored and revealed through that love, and His Kingdom will expand.
When we pray for One there is relational expectation. We fully expect that God will answer our prayers and provide someone for us to love. We become relationally driven as we view every appointment as divine. Praying for One will connect you relationally with others.

When you pray for One you will love your spouse and children more deeply because they are Ones. They are objects of God's love moving through you. When you pray for One, you will become more relationally inclined. You will take relational risks because you desire to be a part of sharing God's love. You will become less concerned about what others can do for you and more concerned about how God can use you as a blessing.

Praying for One changes every relationship you have. It is impossible to view people as you once did. Generally we assign value to people based on what we think they can do for us. That evaluation determines the amount of relational energy we will expend on that person. Praying for One changes that by seeing people primarily as objects of God's love. Their value is that Jesus died for them and that God will love them through us.

Deep relationships are birthed out of deep desires. Valuing others based on what they can do for you is shallow and will only lead to shallow relationships. Praying for One flips a switch and allows you to look at others more deeply. When everyone is seen as a potential object of God's love moving through you, you will experience relational depth and His Kingdom will grow.

THINK ABOUT IT

1. Have you ever been told that you should join a small group at church? If so, why were you encouraged to do so?

2. What are some shallow relational desires? What kind of relationships can you expect to have if your primary relational desires are shallow?

3. What are some deep relational desires? What kind of relationships can you expect to have if your primary relational desires are deep?

4. Churches must have relational depth to be effective in building God's Kingdom. What can you do to foster relational depth in your church?

PRAY ABOUT IT

Ask God to move you through His deep, relational desires. Think through every relationship you have. Ask God to help you view each of those people as Ones. Pray that all of your relationships will reveal God's love and reflect His relational desires.

NOTES:

MISSIONAL

"If you do not know what you are aiming for, you are never going to hit it."

"Aim at nothing and you will probably hit it."

"Keep your eye on the target."

You have probably seen variations of all three of the above quotes. They look great on the inspirational posters featuring cats, sailboats, and majestic mountain scenes that line cubical walls and dentist offices. They are reminders that failing to determine the goal guarantees failure.

In other words, "Failing to plan is planning to fail."

The first step on any journey is to determine where you are going. You cannot have a journey without a destination. **When there is no clear destination, you cannot mark your progress, check to see if you are on course, or be motivated to continue when the going gets tough.** Walking with Jesus is a faith journey and the destination is His missional purpose.

Consider the final words that Jesus spoke to His disciples before ascending into heaven.

> *"But you will receive power when the Holy Spirit comes on you; and you will be my witnesses in Jerusalem, and in all Judea and Samaria, and to the ends of the earth."*
>
> **Acts 1:8**

The power of the Holy Spirit is given for a purpose. Jesus intends for us to be His witnesses. When we refuse to accept and live on mission, it is a tragic abuse and waste of power. Praying for

One reminds us that the gospel is each day's destination and that we live to bear witness to Christ's salvation.

In Ephesians 6 we are told to be strong in the Lord in His mighty power and to put on the full armor of God. The armor includes having feet fitted with the readiness that comes from the gospel of peace. Feet are what move us, and the gospel must advance. There is no retreat or stagnation. We are told to take the sword of the Spirit, which is the Word of God. The Word of God is the gospel. It is the story of Jesus and His salvation. Our feet move us into enemy territory where we wield the sword of the Spirit to set the captives free. Each day is an opportunity to take ground from the enemy by advancing the gospel.

Christians have purpose, but when we refuse to accept and live for that purpose, life becomes miserable fast. Instead of enjoying the journey of life with Jesus, we are stuck in the stagnation that comes from directionless living. Jesus' great and precious promises no longer make sense and are not experienced because we are not on the same path as Him. Christianity without following Jesus is pointless.

Jesus did not die for us so that we could waste our lives in the pursuit of nothing. If you are in Christ, then you are a part of His mission to redeem the world. Never give yourself to less than that. You are a Kingdom-building resource that Jesus longs to unleash on your Ones.

What will you do? Will you pray for One? Will you live today with the aim of reaching the world for Christ? Step out in faith on the greatest missional journey the world has ever known.

THINK ABOUT IT

1. What are you aiming for in life?

2. Have you received the Holy Spirit with power? How do you know?

3. Are your feet fitted with the readiness that comes from the gospel of peace? Are you eager to share the story of Jesus and His salvation?

4. How does God need to adjust your aim? What changes need to be made in order for you to be free to fully embrace the mission of Jesus?

PRAY ABOUT IT

Ask God to give you a plan to pursue His mission. Pray that God would unleash His Church with missional purpose so that the entire world can know Jesus. Pray for One and allow the gospel to be today's destination.

NOTES:

WHY NOT DOUBLE?

chapter seven

WHY NOT DOUBLE?

Throughout history there have been many times when the Church experienced the explosiveness of exponential growth. On day one at Pentecost, the Lord added 3,000 people to their number. Can you imagine the logistical nightmares that came out of that kind of instant growth?

How did the early Church leaders manage the growth and navigate through the messiness that it surely brought?

Initially they did not manage it, and that was a key ingredient to the rapid spread of the gospel. Instead of trying to control the growth, they simply experienced the growth. There were not a lot of thoughts about creating some kind of sustainable infrastructure to maintain individual sets of localized congregations over long periods of time. The focus was on more people in the Kingdom of Heaven, and they fully expected Jesus to return at any given moment.

Time, political pressure, greed, fear, and fatigue have many times knocked the Church off kilter and adjusted the overall aim. God is always faithful to bring the winds of inspiration and revival. When His Body begins to lag in His mission, God shakes things up a bit.

The Holy Spirit stirs within the hearts of believers and they become completely unsatisfied with anything less than God's best. They begin to question. They start to pray expectantly. They visualize lost people being saved. They move beyond the trappings of worldly success and will settle for nothing short of eternal significance.

Then God unleashes His Church for the harvest.

The harvest is plentiful.

Praying for One triggers a release of evangelistic energy that demands exponential growth. One will become two. Two will become four. Four will become eight. As each new person catches the vision to pray for One, he or she is swept up in the momentum of fantastic Kingdom expansion. Suddenly life is no longer about building personal kingdoms because the compulsion to build Christ's Kingdom is dominant.

That is when it starts to get a little scary.

The control freaks among us will begin to panic because they struggle with figuring out how to contain the growth. The less evangelistically-motivated will panic because of feelings of insignificance. The life-long consumers of God begin to panic because they are confronted with the truth that church is not all about them.

People will get concerned that the church is too focused on lost people. Please consider the utter asinine nature of that sentiment. How could Christ's Church ever be too focused on His expressed mission to seek and save the lost?

You can hear the complaints now, can't you?

"What about our needs?"

"What about our children?"

"How are we going to get spiritually fed?"

"We don't want to be a mile wide and an inch deep."

The discomfort will grow as precious resources are utilized more for seeking and saving the lost and less for Christian baby-sitting. Some will not be able to handle it. They have been told for so long that church was about them that the change in aim will be beyond comprehension.

This is precisely why praying for One is so crucial. When the entire church prays for One, everyone gets on board. God makes a directional shift in every heart and mobilizes His Body for purposeful action.

Does it work?

Yes! I have seen it. I am experiencing it.

My church, Manchester Christian Church, prays for One. Our story is valid in demonstrating the effectiveness of praying for One. I will use numbers to help tell this story because numbers are helpful in painting the picture of how God can use a church that prays for One.

The first sermon I preached at Manchester Christian Church was about praying for One. I shared the concept, simplicity, and potential outcome of praying for One. The people connected to the message and were eager to begin praying daily for One.

I told them if we all prayed for One that our church would double in two years. In retrospect that seems like kind of a crazy thing to say on my first Sunday as the Senior Pastor, but I believed it with all my heart.

I am sure that there were some who thought things like: "Oh, isn't that cute? He thinks that our church will double. Doesn't he know that we are already one of the biggest churches in New Hampshire? Doesn't he know that New Hampshire is the least religious state in our country? Doesn't he know that evangelistic work in New Hampshire is like plowing concrete? Doesn't he know that New Englanders are not trusting of outsiders? Doesn't he know that New Englanders are fiercely independent? Doesn't he know that this doubling he speaks of is irrational and impossible? Doesn't he know that he is replacing an amazing Senior Pastor who served here for 30 years? Doesn't he know that studies show that we will most likely experience a 20-40% decrease over the next two years as he begins his ministry here?"

The answer is "yes." Yes, I am cute, and yes, I did know all of those things. I just did not care!

There is a time and place for practical realities to be considered, but praying for One changes reality. I know what God wants to do and what He can do. When people connect to the heart of God through praying for One, growth is the inevitable outcome. The prayer is so compelling because it can be prayed more boldly than any other prayer. Asking God for One person to share His love with is the greatest no brainer in the history of prayer. God's answer is "yes."

On that first Sunday in September, a church committed to pray for One. We accepted the challenge, we started praying right there in the service, and we have not stopped since. Praying for One is mentioned every Sunday and in every email I send our church. When people want to know what we do at Manchester Christian Church, everyone knows that the answer is that we pray for One.

There is synergy, movement, and momentum behind this collective prayer. "Pray for One" has entered our vernacular. People talk openly about their Ones. Everyone has a "pray for One" story. People bring guests and walk around introducing them as their "One." I have even had somebody come up to me on their first Sunday at the church and excitedly proclaim, "I am a One."

Praying for One is FUN! We are having the time of our lives. Church is exciting. People are being saved. Lives are being transformed. The Holy Spirit is working with mighty power. Worship is alive. Joy is the norm. Nobody is the least bit interested in ceasing to pray for One.

But does it work?

Absolutely!

In the first four years of praying for One as a church our weekly attendance almost tripled, the number of campuses tripled, and we baptized over 1,500 people.

Is this kind of growth sustainable? I have no idea, but sustainability is not my primary concern. People are being saved!

When I write that people are being saved, I mean that total life transformation is happening. They are not just becoming church attenders. They are praying for One and are fully-functioning disciples of Jesus who love God, love people, and reproduce spiritually.

Some will argue, "Well, how can you know that? There has not been enough time to determine if true Christian fruit is being exhibited."

I say, "That is a bunch of baloney!"

Where did Christians come up with the ridiculous notion that maturity in Christ can happen only over extended periods of time? Chew on that for a little bit. The Devil has gained a tremendous foothold in our churches by convincing us that only slow growth is good growth. That is totally false. Trust me, from someone who is experiencing it, rapid growth is incredible.

I am not just referring to the rapid growth in numbers. I also mean the rapid growth of Christ in people. We have worked hard to remove the barriers of time from disciple-making by moving from a linear process to an organic experience. Pray for One is a message for everyone. It holds meaning for the thoroughly un-churched and reveals to them what following Christ will entail. It also holds tremendous depth for someone who has been walking with Christ for decades by constantly reminding them of the functional purpose driving their pursuit of Jesus.

The floodgates for rapid growth are thrown open when people are immediately released to participate in building God's Kingdom.

Last year I met a man named Mike. Mike lives near a park downtown where a ministry from our church serves breakfast to homeless and low-income people every Saturday and Sunday. One Sunday, Mike went to the park and had breakfast. While he was there, someone engaged him with the gospel, and Mike surrendered his life to Christ.

After breakfast, he caught a ride to church, and that is when we met. Mike came into our church excited about his new relationship with Jesus. I will never forget meeting him because of the genuine wonder in his eyes. Someone introduced Mike to me, and he said, "Oh, good. You're the Pastor. I was hoping to talk to you because I just had breakfast in the park, and this person told me about Jesus and showed me some things in the Bible. I prayed with them and asked Jesus to be my Lord and Savior. So since I did that, what am I supposed to do now?"

I simply told Mike to pray for One. I told him to ask God to give him One person every day to share the love of Jesus with and then to pay attention to the opportunities that would be before him. Mike said, "I can do that!"

One week later, Mike came bounding into church after breakfast in the park, and he came over to give me an update on his relationship with Jesus. He said, "Ok, you know that praying for One thing you told me to do? Well, I've been doing that, and I woke up this morning and thought, you know what? Those people who shared Jesus with me were probably praying for One, and they go to the park to serve breakfast every Saturday and Sunday, so I'll go to the park and do what they do. So, I got out of bed and went down to the park to volunteer. They put me right to work, and I had my first Sunday as a volunteer in the Do You Know Him? Ministry. So, what do I do now?"

I told Mike to keep praying for One, and he said, "Can do, Pastor Bo!" and he marched off.

The very next Sunday, Mike showed up at church even more excited than he had been the previous two weeks. He could barely contain himself as he waited in line to speak with me. I could see him behind a couple of people bouncing up and down with a huge smile on his face. When he finally got to talk to me, he could hardly contain himself.

Mike said, "So, I've been doing that pray for One thing like you told me, and this morning I went to the park to serve in my

181

volunteer position with the Do You Know Him? Ministry. I met this lady who didn't know Jesus, so I sat down with her and told her what the people told me two weeks ago. I showed her what they showed me in the Bible, and then she prayed to give her life to Christ. So I got my first One today. What do I do next?"

Can you guess what I told him? That's right. I simply said, "Pray for another One." And that's exactly what Mike is doing.

Not long after that, Mike and I baptized his wife together. Every time I see Mike, he has a testimony to share. Recently he has been delivered from alcoholism. To date, Mike is four months sober. He loves telling people that he used to drink and how Jesus is changing his life. Mike shares God's love with me and with everyone he meets. He is a Praying for One machine.

God uses people like Mike. Mike is the type of guy that the world generally places little value in. He would probably be the guy that would get picked last for kickball in elementary school. He wouldn't be described as smart, wealthy, talented, handsome, and so on. But that is not what God is looking for. Mike has the best characteristic of all...he is available.

It was two weeks from the time Mike was saved until he led his first One to Christ. Two weeks! How long has it been for you?

I am so glad that we were able to give Mike clear direction on what to do next. More people are in the Kingdom of Heaven because Jesus captivated Mike's heart. We did not tell Mike to get off alcohol, clean up his language, join a Bible study group, take a series of classes, and so on. We just told Mike to pray for One. That's what he is doing, but guess what? On his own, Mike has decided to get off alcohol, clean up his language, join a Bible study group, and take classes. He wants to do all those things so that he is more effective at sharing God's love with each and every One God puts in his path.

I cannot tell the story of what God is doing in Manchester Christian Church without sharing stories like Mike's. We have tons of them because the exponential growth we are experiencing is all driven by praying for One. Our church doubled in size in two years because we pray for One.

Churches grow for lots of reasons. Sometimes the growth comes from the completion of a building project, the introduction of a dynamic new ministry, the failing of another church, and so on. Often leaders cannot articulate why their church is growing.

We know why Manchester Christian Church is growing... we pray for One, but we also make a way for One.

I see no valid reason to inhibit a church's growth. Why not pray, plan, and prepare to double? If everyone in your church is praying for One, shouldn't you expect exponential growth?

There are practical realities to consider. The most obvious and most often neglected issue regarding church growth is the number of available seats. Here's the deal. People (churched or un-churched) want to attend worship services on Sundays between 9:00 and 11:00 a.m. I am not saying that there is no value in alternate worship times (Saturday, etc.), but the practical reality is that people are most likely to attend church between 9:00 and 11:00 a.m. on Sunday mornings. Simple logic dictates that if you are going to pray for One and double every couple of years, then you are going to need twice as many seats.

It's simple and obvious, but I missed it in the past. Before becoming the Senior Pastor at Manchester Christian Church, I was a failed church planter. People hate the word "fail" in the context of church, but the fact of the matter is that our church plant failed. We started a church from scratch with the intention of growing a dynamic body of Christ-followers that would impact the community for generations to come.

That church plant no longer exists though, so by definition it failed. We failed. Don't get me wrong. We know that God did many wonderful things through the church plant. There were many people who were saved, and life change occurred. I don't want to diminish that, but by the same token, I'm not comfortable ignoring how my leadership flaws and other factors stopped the church from growing and led to its ultimate demise.

Like most church planters, I had a big vision. We did some prelaunch meetings, and God drew a group of people together that was inspired to change a region. The church began in an elementary school and had 150 people attending from almost day one. Within two months of starting the church, God laid the concept of Pray for One on my heart. I began to share it passionately with the church, and the people eagerly jumped at the opportunity to be active participants in building God's Kingdom.

Everyone was praying for One, and sure enough, we began to grow. I had studied and prepared for church planting. I knew the statistics about how large a plant could grow in different types of facilities. I knew that churches meeting in elementary schools rarely grew above 200 members, and the average attendance was much, much lower. The only facility available to us was an elementary school, and sure enough, we reached a point of repulsion quickly. We would have a Sunday with 185 in attendance, then drop to 160 the following Sunday, and then slowly creep back up to 185 to 200 before contracting again.

I understood the practical reality of our situation, but I assumed that we would be different. For some crazy reason, I thought that our church plant would be the exception to the rule, so we just pressed forward thinking that we could double to 400 people in that elementary school. Oops! The validity of the Praying for One message remained, but our people stopped actually doing it. They knew that praying for One could work because God brought people into their lives to share His love with, but practically speaking, there was no room in our church for any more Ones.

The people would nod and smile in agreement as each Sunday I reminded everyone to pray for One, but it did not take long for them to realize subconsciously that praying for One without making a way for One is essentially pointless. Since this was the primary messaging and methodology for our church, I basically lost all leadership credibility. The people still liked me. They liked the church. But like does not translate into personal buy in.

After suffering several facility let downs over a few years, we decided that it was time to stop playing pretend and deal with reality. Praying for One cannot work without having room for One.

Now for the cynically minded reader who thinks seats do not matter and that large churches are not the answer, I would like for you to consider the Parable of the Talents found in Matthew 25:14-30.

"Again, it will be like a man going on a journey, who called his servants and entrusted his property to them. To one he gave five talents of money, to another two talents, and to another one talent, each according to his ability. Then he went on his journey. The man who had received the five talents went at once and put his money to work and gained five more. So also, the one with the two talents gained two more. But the man who had received the one talent went off, dug a hole in the ground and hid his master's money.

"After a long time the master of those servants returned and settled accounts with them. The man who had received the five talents brought the other five. 'Master,' he said, 'you entrusted me with five talents. See, I have gained five more.'

"His master replied, 'Well done, good and faithful servant! You have been faithful with a few things; I will put you in charge of many things. Come and share your master's happiness!'

"The man with the two talents also came. 'Master,' he said, 'you entrusted me with two talents; see, I have gained two more.'

"His master replied, 'Well done, good and faithful servant! You have been faithful with a few things; I will put you in charge of many things. Come and share your master's happiness!'

"Then the man who had received the one talent came. 'Master,' he said, 'I knew that you are a hard man, harvesting where you have not sown and gathering where you have not scattered seed. So I was afraid and went out and hid your talent in the ground. See, here is what belongs to you.'

"His master replied, 'You wicked, lazy servant! So you knew that I harvest where I have not sown and gather where I have not scattered seed? Well then, you should have put my money on deposit with the bankers, so that when I returned I would have received it back with interest.

"'Take the talent from him and give it to the one who has the ten talents. For everyone who has will be given more, and he will have an abundance. Whoever does not have, even what he has will be taken from him. And throw that worthless servant outside, into the darkness, where there will be weeping and gnashing of teeth.'"

It is the responsibility of every local church to reach as many people as possible. They must leverage every resource at their disposal for the purpose of seeing more people in the Kingdom of Heaven. Sometimes churches that want to appear deep, bury their talents. Can you imagine standing before Jesus at judgment and giving an account for a church that refused to build the Kingdom?

What would you say? Would it be something like this?

"Hey, Jesus. We are really excited to see you here. We took the people you entrusted us with, and we got them really deep into your Word. Now we didn't actually reach any new people, but the ones we started with are a lot better at worship, Bible study, long flowing prayers, and their sin management skills are impeccable. So, how did we do?"

Hmm...how did we do?

So many churches play it safe. They batten down the hatches and try to hold on in survival mode. Instead of risking it all to see more people in the Kingdom of Heaven, they bury their talents deep because they are afraid. The only things we ought to be burying are dead things. Churches that bury their talents are dead.

But hey! God is in the resurrection business, right?

Praying for One and making a way for One can resurrect any church.

These lessons on dealing with practical realities were not lost on me. When I became the Senior Pastor at Manchester Christian Church, I carried with me the knowledge of how ignoring the need for something as simple as more seats can totally kill a church's momentum. When 1,200 people committed to pray for One, I knew that we needed find a way to make room for 2,400 people.

When there were 2,400 people praying for One, we knew that we needed to make a way for there to be seats for 4,800 people.

We committed our best minds to this problem of always having enough seats to continue praying for One and landed on a multi-site strategy. Being one church in multiple locations allows for an unlimited amount of seats. Of course there is cost involved in this, but one of the best parts about praying for One is that the people are all responsible.

When I needed to stand up in front of Manchester Christian Church to raise money for more seats, it was easy. I simply told the church that we were doubling and that it was all their fault. I reminded them that the growth was the result of praying for One and that we had no intention of not praying for One, so we better pull together and make a way for One. They opened their hearts and their wallets, and in one year we went from one site to three so that there could be enough seats for us to continue praying for One.

So, why not double? Honestly, there are lots of reasons not to double. Sometimes circumstances are just out of our control. I don't know what tomorrow holds. A fire, a scandal, a split, or just plain old-fashioned poor leadership could wipe out Manchester Christian Church.

All I know is that I believe with all my heart that if we pray for One and make a way for One, then there will be more people in the Kingdom of Heaven. We should never settle for less, and if Christians would just keep doubling, the whole world could be reached with the love of Jesus!

FEAR

It is perfectly reasonable to expect a church that prays for One to double in size. When a local congregation prays for One, God opens the doors for His love, grace, and mercy to flow. People get saved and evangelistic momentum builds.

As the church fulfills its functional purpose, people are encouraged and emboldened to participate in building God's Kingdom. Things will snowball quickly, and many find this scary. Rapid growth triggers fear because of the changes that unfold. Praying for One transforms the church in many ways, and being aware of the fears that you and others might face on this journey is helpful for overcoming them and trusting God.

It is crazy to think that we might allow a little thing like fear to keep us from fulfilling God's mission for His Church, but fear is one of the biggest obstacles to overcome. I have always found that one of the best ways to deal with fear is by naming it. We fear the unknown, and when what we fear is ambiguous, it has greater power over us. **Naming fears allows us to determine how valid the threat really is and helps in setting a plan of action to overcome the fear.**

So, what do we fear in regard to our church doubling in size and growing rapidly?

We fear change.

A church that prays for One will change. As people become consumed with the mission of Jesus, the programming changes. The church will use its resources to reach people with the gospel. This produces discomfort for anyone not praying for One because they do not understand it. They want things to stay the same. In their minds, their church exists to meet their needs. They bought into the lie that the church is supposed to revolve around them. They shopped long and hard to find the best possible church. You know the church: with the type of preaching they like, the kind of music they like, the best programs for their kids, and the one that has other people who look, act, and think just like them. Praying for One changes all of that. When you pray for One, your only concern in being a part of a local church is thinking about where you can reach the most people for Jesus.

We fear sacrifice.

Praying for One always leads to sacrifice. Reaching people is costly. You can ask God about that. He so loved the world that He gave His one and only Son. Churches that pray for One and prepare for exponential growth must sacrifice. You will sacrifice your personal desires, agendas, time, and finances in order to reach your Ones. Sacrifice is a scary thing, and those who do not pray for One, will not understand. I have heard it said that sacrifice is giving up something you love for something you love more. Praying for One puts the mission of Jesus at the forefront of the heart, and sacrifice becomes a normal expression of faith to build God's Kingdom.

We fear the loss of control.

Dynamic church growth produces an uncontrollable situation. How will we control all of these new people? How can we make sure that they all do what they are supposed to do? How can we meet all of their needs? Exponential growth really is impossible to manage. The church must take the risk of allowing the Holy Spirit to be in charge. Imagine the day at Pentecost when 3,000 people became new followers of Jesus.

"Those who accepted his message were baptized, and about three thousand were added to their number that day."

Acts 2:41

Can you imagine the logistical nightmare of 3,000 new believers in one day? What if your church reached 3,000 new people next Sunday? Movements of God are experienced, not controlled. We are called to participate in what He is doing and should never allow fear to stop the work of the Holy Spirit.

Praying for One puts fear in check. The desire for more people in the Kingdom of Heaven overrides the many fears that well up. Risk becomes normative as the church leverages all its resources to reach the most people in the shortest time. Do not be afraid.

THINK ABOUT IT

1. What are some things that churches have been afraid to change in order to reach more people?

2. Do you have any fears about praying for One? Are you afraid of who God might ask you to share His love with or sacrifices you may need to make?

3. What does God say about fear? Should we allow fear to be a primary motivator?

4. What do you think praying for One will cost you?

PRAY ABOUT IT

Acknowledge your fears to God. Ask Him to help you to trust Him. Pray for your church to be a local body of believers who are all in for the mission of Jesus. Consider what praying for One might cost you and submit yourself to God's will.

NOTES:

EXPECTATIONS

We all carry expectations. Faulty expectations produce disappointment. Appropriate expectations prepare us for success.

Christians often carry many faulty expectations.

We think that if we obey God bad things will not happen to us. This expectation is a recipe for disappointment. Jesus did not promise His followers pain-free lives. In fact, He said the opposite.

> *"I have told you these things, so that in me you may have peace. In this world you will have trouble. But take heart! I have overcome the world."*
>
> **John 16:33**

Jesus wants His followers to have appropriate expectations. He warns us that following Him will often lead us into trouble. Life will not be all rainbows, candy canes, and lollipops. We are called to follow Jesus and do what He did. Jesus laid down His life and told us to do the same.

> *"Whoever does not take up their cross and follow me is not worthy of me. Whoever finds their life will lose it, and whoever loses their life for my sake will find it."*
>
> **Matthew 10:38-39**

Life with Jesus is an adventurous journey. It is filled with passion, purpose, and power. There is meaning in the pain that is experienced. None of it is wasted. God reveals Himself through His followers and draws others into His Kingdom. It is truly a life worth living. Jesus' admonition to "take heart" is one that all of His followers should eagerly cling to daily. He has indeed overcome the world, and we will as well.

But we must have proper expectations.

Praying for One sets Christ's purpose in the hearts of His followers. When our predominant prayer is to fulfill His mission, we genuinely begin to seek His will. **Life can no longer be a charade of pain avoidance. Christians will throw themselves headlong into trouble when it means that people will be saved.** Christians joyfully sacrifice when it means that people will be saved. Christians faithfully steward the resources of time, talents, and treasures when they know that more people will be in the Kingdom of Heaven.

This is why it is critical for local churches to have the heartbeat of Jesus. Praying for One is good on the individual level, but it is great at the group level. When Christians have appropriate expectations for the church, they are set up for amazing Kingdom success. There is an understanding that the church is the light of the world. It is a city on a hill. The church is to shine and draw the lost and weary home. Success is measured in people being saved because that is the communal expectation.

People are often disappointed with their local church. Over the years I have heard numerous disappointments expressed. People say things like, the preacher is boring, the music is too loud, the youth group is not big enough, I'm not being fed, and so on. Churchgoers almost never express disappointment by saying, "Our church isn't reaching lost people."

If your church will pray for One, they will expect people to be saved. Appropriate expectations lead to success. When the expectation is right, God moves through His people to do great things. The Kingdom of Heaven will grow exponentially as God's people refuse to settle for less than His best.

THINK ABOUT IT

1. What do you think churchgoers expect from their churches? List the top three expectations.

2. What does Jesus expect from His Church? Do you think that Jesus' expectations match the common churchgoers' expectations?

3. What disappointments have you experienced or heard from others regarding being a part of a local church? What do you think produced those disappointments? Were there faulty expectations involved?

4. Imagine if everyone in your church prayed for One. What would your church look like if the primary communal expectation of the church were to reach the world for Christ? What would change?

PRAY ABOUT IT

Confess any faulty expectations you have. Ask God to reveal false expectations that are hidden in your heart. Pray for One and allow God's expectation to set you up for success. Take heart! Jesus has overcome the world.

NOTES:

MATURITY

There is a fallacy in many Christian circles that spiritual maturity can only occur over extended periods of time.

This simply is not true.

Rapid spiritual transformation is a biblical norm that ought to be expected in our churches. The New Testament is full of stories about people who had encounters with Jesus and were radically changed on the spot.

The Woman at the Well in John 4 meets Jesus, and on the same day testifies to her entire village that He is the Christ.

The apostle Paul in Acts 9 was blinded by Jesus on the road to Damascus, and after having his vision restored and being baptized, he at once began to preach that Jesus is the Son of God. Paul went from persecuting the Church to building the Church in three days.

In Luke 19, Zacchaeus climbs a tree in order to see Jesus. Jesus invites Himself to dinner at Zacchaeus' house. People muttered about Jesus hanging out with an awful, tax-collecting sinner like Zacchaeus, but on that same day Zacchaeus stood up for Jesus and gave half of his possessions to the poor and paid back four times the amount he had cheated people out of.

In Acts 8, the Ethiopian Eunuch heard the gospel from Philip and responded by declaring that he should be baptized. There was no waiting period, no series of classes to attend, no hoops to jump through. Philip explained who Jesus is and the Ethiopian Eunuch saw some water and was baptized on the spot.

The disciples only knew Jesus for three years before He entrusted them with His mission. They received the Holy Spirit in Acts 2 and immediately began to preach. The result was pretty positive…3,000 people were saved that day!

I personally cannot stand it when people label new believers as "baby Christians." It is condescending and perpetuates the myth that maturity only happens over time. There are people who have spent lifetimes in churches and do not possess a lick of authentic spiritual maturity. They are bitter, hateful, resentful, prideful, and foolish. The fruit of the Spirit is not present, yet there is some demented belief that they are mature in Christ because they have put in their time at church.

Time does not equal maturity.

Lordship and surrender to the Holy Spirit are what produce mature believers. There is no reason to believe that this cannot happen quickly. When we release people to live for Jesus and build His Kingdom, the results are fantastic. Christianity is not difficult to understand or explain. In fact, Jesus said that we are to have child-like faith.

> *"He called a little child to him, and placed the child among them. And he said: 'Truly I tell you, unless you change and become like little children, you will never enter the kingdom of heaven. Therefore, whoever takes the lowly position of this child is the greatest in the kingdom of heaven.'"*
> **Matthew 18:2-4**

When there is an expectation that rapid maturity and growth will occur, people respond. Put the gospel in their hands and set them loose to reproduce spiritually. Stop making simple things complicated. Drop the pretenses of church hierarchy and let Jesus work miracles in people.

In fact, why not let Jesus work a miracle in you? What's stopping you from being radically transformed today? You do not need to wait years and years to become a mature follower of Jesus. The marks of maturity in Christ are loving God, loving people, and reproducing spiritually.

Pray for One and watch what happens. Praying for One sets the stage for rapid growth in Christ because the predominant desire becomes building His Kingdom, and we refuse to settle for less.

THINK ABOUT IT

1. Are you a mature or maturing Christian? How do you know?

2. How do you think the common belief that maturity only happens over time holds people back from transformational growth in Christ?

3. Disciples of Jesus make disciples of Jesus. If you are in Christ, how is Jesus using you to make more disciples?

4. What is holding you back from experiencing transformational growth today?

PRAY ABOUT IT

Ask God to give you and your church His perspective on maturity in Christ. Seek Him to understand His will for His followers. Ask God to reveal any attitudes or beliefs in you that stifle maturity. Pray for a miracle of radical transformation in your life today.

NOTES:

OBSTACLES

It is fun and exciting to be part of a local church where people are getting saved on a daily basis. There is a shared sense of urgency within the church to reach people, and there is a stubborn refusal to settle for less than God's best. The church is alive and passionate when new people are responding to the gospel. Momentum builds with each life that is redeemed and set apart for God's purpose.

Praying for One creates a shared expectation and desire for exponential Kingdom impact. A local church that prays for One is unified around the mission of Jesus to seek and save the lost. There is great power in shared vision.

Leadership is emboldened to take on obstacles with confidence and hope. Praying for One does not remove obstacles that prevent growth, but it does position the church to deal with growth barriers efficiently and expeditiously. The shared aspect of the church praying a unified prayer positions the church to overcome barriers by leveraging the collective power of the people.

There is nothing in this world as powerful as the local church. We have Kingdom authority to storm the gates of Hell to set the captives free. The Church prevails. Jesus wins. Ultimate victory is His, so why not dwell in daily victory as well?

There will always be obstacles to growing God's Kingdom. We ought to expect it and rejoice in the face of adversity. When the going gets tough, the Church gets going! The local church does its best work under pressure. When resources are stretched, when the deck is stacked against us, when everyone is needed to pull off the God-sized vision the church has decided to pursue...that's when the local church is at its best.

"Rejoice in the Lord always. I will say it again: Rejoice! Let your gentleness be evident to all. The Lord is near. Do not be anxious about anything, but in every situation, by prayer and petition, with thanksgiving, present your requests to God. And the peace of God, which transcends all understanding, will guard your hearts and your minds in Christ Jesus."

Philippians 4:4-7

Many people cling to faulty theology that promotes the notion that if we are in God's will, then there will be no difficulties. They sit back and passively wait for God to open doors or quickly abandon worthwhile endeavors over simple problems. Entire generations of God's people have wasted precious opportunities, sitting on the sidelines of faith, when they should have been advancing into enemy territory proclaiming the salvation of Jesus.

Too many Christians view the gospel of Christ like a velvet lifeline that we occasionally extend to the poor, suffering saps below in hopes that someone might grab hold and be lured to freedom. **The gospel is not a velvet lifeline. It is a battering ram that demolishes strongholds and every pretense set in opposition to the heart of God.** The gospel is the sword of the Spirit, and we are called to advance the Kingdom with warrior-like zeal.

Praying for One sets our hearts ablaze with the mission of Jesus. We are compelled to sacrifice and overcome obstacles. There is a shared sense of opportunity as the church is moved from entitlement to responsibility. We understand the gravity of what is entrusted to us.

I implore you to pray for One, but do not do it alone. Share this with your family, friends, and church. Pray together for

God to give each of you One to share His love with. Talk about obstacles and strategize together to overcome anything in the way of people knowing the Way.

THINK ABOUT IT

1. What are some common obstacles that you personally face in sharing Jesus with others?

2. What prevents churches from seeking and saving the lost? What are some practical issues that must be overcome to reach the most people in the shortest time?

3. Can you see the collective power found in the local church praying for One? What benefits are there for the Kingdom when believers pray with united hearts?

4. What is your personal attitude toward obstacles? How could praying for One help you to recognize when God is leading you to demolish obstacles to set the captives free?

PRAY ABOUT IT

Pray for your local church. Ask God to unite the church around His mission. Pray that the church will faithfully utilize every resource available to expand God's Kingdom. Ask God to use you to reach Ones who do not know Him yet.

NOTES:

RISKY BUSINESS

chapter eight

RISKY BUSINESS

Praying for One is not safe. It is not cheap. It is not all sunshine, rainbows, and lollipops.

Praying for One is risky. It is not for the faint of heart. Those content with the status quo need not apply.

Praying for One will destroy the mental checklist of all the things that you will not do for God that you carry close to your heart for personal protection. It will lead you to throw caution to the wind. You will go places no self-righteous Christian would ever go. You will have conversations that would cause the easily offended to blush with indignant shame. You will touch people that most churches at best would simply just ignore or at worst would point the bony finger of judgment at and shout, "Unclean!"

Praying for One moves you to the lunatic fringe. It takes you out of the realm of cultural Christianity and moves you into the divine flow of Holy Spirit action. Simply put, when you pray for One, it is going to get crazy.

Crazy is good. Following Jesus is supposed to be crazy. It should be dangerous. It ought to be wild and adventurous. Christianity is an out-of-this-world experience. Christ followers are strangers and aliens on this earth. This place is not our home. We serve as ambassadors for a better home...a heavenly home. That mission gets lost when we get comfortable in this time and place.

Praying for One draws attention Heavenward. It lifts the believer out of the emptiness of Christian clichés and into raging depths of Christ's love. Christians are notorious for spouting clever little sayings designed to placate and console. We say things like, "The safest place in the world to be is at the center of God's will." Hmm...safe? I don't think so. It is not safe at all.

Safe? No. Good? Yes.

There is no promise of personal protection in following Jesus. That thought alone is enough to rock some to their theological core. Many hold a foundational belief that God would never allow anything "bad" to happen to them. They may not verbalize it, but the ideology is there. This type of thinking blocks the effectiveness of praying for One.

When the primary worldview is one of self-preservation, praying for One is rendered essentially impotent. We need to understand right up front that seeking and saving the lost is dangerous work. Simple logic ought to confirm this line of thinking.

Christians are Christ followers. That means that we do what Jesus did.

What did Jesus do? He came to this earth and gave His life as a ransom for many. Jesus explicitly told us to take up our crosses and follow Him. He told us that whoever wants to save his life will lose it, but whoever loses his life for Christ's sake will gain eternity.

Why would we ever think that following Jesus would produce different results for us than it did for Him and His first disciples? Are we more favored? Are we better? Has the mission changed?

The mission has not changed and the stakes are still just as high. Is this scary? Absolutely, but I can tell you from experience that it beats the Hell out not living for Jesus. (FYI...there is no need to be offended...Hell was used in the appropriate biblical sense in the previous sentence and not as a curse word...Hell is separation from God, and living for Jesus conquers Hell...you can do the math.)

Yeah, but...

No.

Let's keep our buts to ourselves. I know that we have some really big buts. Sometimes we like our big buts more than we like the truth of Jesus.

I cannot lie; the issue of "buts" is a struggle. What I have found, though, is that praying for One helps me overcome my objections to following Jesus. He counters my big buts with a better hope. I have no need to build a personal kingdom when I am sharing in His eternal Kingdom!

One of my early pray for One encounters put this notion of risk to the test. It was during my church planting days when a man named Steve walked into our Sunday service for the first time. We were meeting in a bar in a soccer stadium at the time, and Steve came in just after the service started and sat alone on the front row. Our little church was extremely tuned in to welcoming guests, so despite his best efforts to go unnoticed, we were all very aware of his presence.

Steve began to cry very soon after finding his seat, and he continued crying through the entire service. After the closing song, we gave him a moment or two to compose himself before we pounced. He was welcomed, introduced around, given information about the church, and loved on in a very sincere fashion.

Steve returned the following Sunday and proceeded to cry through the service a second time. On that day, I had the opportunity to hear a little bit of his story. Steve was recently divorced. He was in financial ruin. Alcohol had a major grip on him.

Steve's world was in utter chaos. The first half of his life had been spent chasing financial gain. He lived by himself in a big house. He drove a sports car he could not afford. He had expensive taste in clothes and jewelry. Image was everything, but he had nothing. Debt was crushing him, and the pressures of life had become unmanageable.

When Steve came to church for the third week in a row, I asked if he would like to have lunch one day. He agreed to meet me two days latter. He also picked up a copy of a book I had written and told me that he would start reading it along with the Bible to help pull him through the week.

We met for lunch on a Tuesday, and I could tell that Steve was still pretty skeptical about the whole church thing. I decided to take a blatantly honest approach with him. I shared my struggles with him. I listened intently to all that he was facing. I pointed him to Jesus. Steve agreed that we should continue the conversation, and he told me that he had started reading my book. I gave him my cell phone number and told him to text or call anytime.

Steve sent me a text message two days later at 9:30 p.m. The text read, "I'm on page 54. Come over."

Now let me tell you...I lead a pretty exciting life. I mean, I like the nightlife...I like to party, but on this particular Thursday night I was in my pajamas and had closed up shop for the night. My wife and kids were snuggled in bed, and I was watching a little television before calling it a night myself.

I had no idea where Steve lived, and I had no intention of going to his house by myself after 10:00 p.m. But before responding to his text message, I prayed for him. After all, I was praying for One, and there was little doubt that Steve was an answer to prayer. As I prayed, I felt the urge to look up page 54 in the book I had written. I flipped open the book and realized that Steve was reading about how we must surrender everything to God and receive Jesus as Lord.

Here is page 54 in its entirety.

We preach freedom and live in bondage. We proclaim life and dwell in death. Christians are tired, angry, and frustrated because we choose to carry burdens we are not meant to hold. The journey is hard enough on its own; we don't need the added weight of baggage.

Jesus wants to strip us of this heavy load so that we can follow Him. If we follow Him, we live. If we live, He is glorified. Put your burden down. You don't really need it. Jesus is sufficient.

One of the things that I love about Jesus is that He always seems to do things in an 'over-the-top' fashion. He always goes above and beyond.

Like, in this case, He doesn't just want us to surrender our burdens to Him. He offers a trade-in.

Jesus promises to give us everything that we need. He says that when we keep in step with the Spirit, then certain things will be produced. It is called fruit. Perhaps you have heard of the fruit of the Spirit. This fruit is love, joy, peace, patience, kindness, goodness, faithfulness, gentleness, and self-control. All of these produce freedom.

So, if we lay our burdens down and follow Jesus, He gives us a new reality. He takes our junk and replaces it with life. We are no longer burdened but free.

Think about it.

(I'm Going to Light Myself on Fire,
Bo Chancey, p. 54)

As soon as I read that, I knew that I had to go to Steve's house. He was ready to surrender his life to Christ, and he wanted me to share in that most sacred moment. I sent Steve a text message asking where he lived. It turned out that he only lived about two miles away from me. I let him know that I would be over ASAP, and that was when it got risky.

I walked upstairs into the master bedroom and started to put some clothes on. My wife said, "What are you doing?"

I replied, "I'm going over to Steve's house."

She asked, "Who is Steve?"

I said, "You know, the guy I had lunch with on Tuesday."

She said, "No, I do not know that guy. Who is Steve?"

I said, "You know...he's the guy that has come to church the last three weeks, sits on the front row, and cries through the service."

She said, "No, I do not know him. Who is Steve?"

I said, "I told you about him. He's the lonely guy who is recently divorced, addicted to alcohol, facing bankruptcy, and is really depressed."

She said, "Oh...so what makes you think that going to his house alone at 10:00 on a Thursday night is a good idea?"

I said, "He's on page 54."

She said, "What's page 54?"

I said, "It's about surrender. Steve wants to give his life to Christ. He wants me to come over and pray with him."

She asked, "Can't that wait until tomorrow?"

I said, "No! He's ready right now. I have to go."

She said, "You are not going over there alone tonight."

I asked, "Why not?"

She said, "It's too dangerous. You don't know this guy. You don't know anybody who knows this guy. He is depressed, under the influence of alcohol, and is highly unpredictable. You can't go."

Now just to be clear. My wife often serves as the voice of reason in our relationship. I listen to her. God uses her more in my life than any other human. I respect her and the points she made were absolutely valid. Our relationship is filled with mutual trust and respect. Normally I would have totally conceded to her wishes, but this was different. This was a pray for One moment.

I told her, "I have to go."

She said, "I am not okay with you going to his house. If you have to go, call him and see if he will meet you for coffee. That way I know that you are safe and are in a public setting."

Seeing that this was a perfectly reasonable alternative, I agreed to call him to set up a place to meet.

I called Steve and said, "Let's go grab some coffee and talk."

Steve said, "No. I'm already on my fifth beer. Come over because there is something that I need to give to you."

For some crazy reason this made sense to me so I said, "Okay, I'll be there in ten minutes."

I went back into the bedroom and told my wife what Steve had said. The fact that Steve was on beer number five did not comfort her in the least, but she knew that I was going to his house.

She rolled over in bed and said, "Well, I guess if you are going to die, getting shot by a lonely, depressed drunk guy in his house late at night because he is on page 54 of your book is about as good a way to go as any."

I kissed her on the head, and she said, "Send me a text message in an hour or so to let me know if you are not dead."

That final sentence my wife said to me really stuck in my head. The whole way over to Steve's house, I prayed for him, but I also got fixated on how he might kill me. The reality that I did not know this guy and that he was really unstable started to mess with my head. As I prayed, I made a decision that if it was time to die, then I would die for Jesus. I know that seems dramatic, but that was the state of mind I was in when I arrived at Steve's house.

I pulled into Steve's driveway, and he was waiting for me in his garage. I was kind of hoping that maybe we could just stay outside and talk, but he immediately had me follow him inside. We walked into his kitchen, and he popped open another beer. Steve was different than I had seen him on other occasions. He was calm. His words were steady, and his thoughts were clear. The difference in him was a bit unnerving.

We stood at the bar in his kitchen, and he thanked me for coming over. He said that he wanted to surrender his life to Christ and that he had something to give me. I asked him if he wanted to pray together, and he said, "Yes." We prayed, and Steve asked Jesus to be his Lord and Savior.

When we finished praying, Steve told me why page 54 had such an impact on him. He said that he had spent his entire adult life trying to be successful through the accumulation of stuff. Possessions and status symbols were his gods. He told me that he collected expensive watches and that there was one watch in particular that was his favorite. He said that it was the first big-ticket item he had ever purchased and that, of all his watches, it was the one that most symbolized his life up to that point. Since he was starting a new life with Christ, he wanted to give me that watch, and he asked if I would pray for him each time I put it on.

I was nervous about accepting such an expensive and meaningful gift, but his eyes expressed a sincerity and genuineness that I could not deny. I told him that I would take the watch on two conditions. The first was that, if at any time he wanted it back, I would return it to him with no questions asked. The second was that I would pray for him when I put it on, but he would have to agree to pray for One whenever he put his watch on. Steve agreed to both conditions and then told me to follow him into the closet in his master bedroom where he kept his safe.

As we walked through his bedroom, I spotted a shotgun sticking out from behind his bed. The sight of that gun sent a surge of panic through me as I remembered my wife's comments about dying, and I thought about a scene from a movie I had just seen.

I had recently watched a movie where a couple of thieves had double-crossed each other. In the final scene, one thief had the other at gunpoint and forced him to open a floor safe where the stolen money was stashed. With one last plot twist, the guy at gunpoint reached into the safe, pulled out a hidden gun, and shot the other thief.

As we moved through Steve's bathroom and into his closet, I became certain that I was about to die. I just knew that, as he bent down to open the safe, he would pull a gun out and shoot me. My heart was racing. I had totally psyched myself out. I had forgotten all about the watch, so when he took it out and turned to hand it to me, I was on my heels backing up and out of the closet. He looked at me kind of strangely as my arms were raised near my chest in a symbolic gesture of surrender. Steve extended the watch to me and said, "Here…try it on."

The fact that he was holding a watch and not a gun brought tremendous relief. I placed the watch on my wrist as Steve told me all about why the watch was so valuable to him. This was a huge moment for him, but it was also a major turning point for me. The risk involved in praying for One had become a reality.

Steve and I went into his living room and sat down on his couches to continue our chat. My wife sent me a text message to see if I was still alive. While I was responding to her, Steve realized how late it was and that I was married. He immediately started apologizing for getting me out of my house so late at night, and he asked if my wife was angry with me.

I said, "No, she is not angry. She is worried and scared."

Steve got a really confused look on his face as he tried to figure out why my wife would be worried. I saw him trying to mentally connect the dots, and then it clicked. Steve said, "Oh… tell her I'm not gay!"

I said, "Buddy, that's the least of her worries."

He looked confused again.

When I told him that she was afraid that he was going to kill me, he started to laugh. I chuckled too but confessed that I had been pretty rattled by the whole encounter. I told him that, when I saw the shotgun sticking out from behind his bed, I was convinced I was about to be shot.

Steve got a kick out of that then proceeded to tell me that he had only fired that shotgun once inside his house. He took me into the dining room where there was a shotgun blast through the wall. He told me that he had been ready to kill himself but decided not to at the last minute, so he just shot a hole through the wall instead.

I explained to Steve that, with his history of depression, keeping a loaded gun in the house was a bad idea. We prayed together and each asked God to give us One person to share His love with. Then I went home to a relieved wife.

Steve continues to pray for One, and he has shared the love of Jesus with tons of people. I have worn that watch every day for years, and when I look at it, I think about Steve and how praying for One is changing me. I take risks that I wouldn't have before, and life is much more exciting.

Praying for One is going to pull you out of your comfort zone. It will inconvenience you. It will cost you. It will transform you.

You will speak with people you would have never spoken to before. You will touch people you would have otherwise ignored. Jesus will conquer fears, insecurities, and prejudices within you. Excuses will be replaced with expectant prayers for One to share God's love with.

And God's Kingdom will grow.

DANGEROUS

Following Jesus is going to entail some risk. It is insane to expect otherwise.

Christians, by definition, are followers of Jesus, and He led a pretty dangerous life. Jesus did not try to maintain the status quo. He never played it safe. Jesus ruffled feathers, upset political and religious powers, and knowingly positioned Himself to be executed.

Hey, I've got a great idea…let's follow that guy!

It is totally wrong to assume that following Jesus will never lead you into dangerous places. Safety is not at the top of Jesus' list and therefore should not be at the top of yours. It is impossible to produce Kingdom- building fruit when safety is a top priority. Evaluating God's will based on personal safety guarantees failure.

The first disciples certainly struggled with this. They were preparing to fight a physical battle to establish an earthly kingdom for the Jewish people. They envisioned the Messiah as a military, conquering king who would overthrow the Roman government. Try to imagine how insanely difficult it was for them to follow Jesus as He prepared to die.

There was no way that Jesus' plan of self-sacrifice could have made sense to them, yet they were compelled to follow Him even when walking into the face of obvious danger. In John 8, Jesus claims to be God. The religious leaders heard this and considered it blasphemous and punishable by death.

> *"Very truly I tell you,' Jesus answered, 'before Abraham was born, I am!' At this, they picked up stones to stone him, but Jesus hid himself, slipping away from the temple grounds."*

John 8:58-59

The disciples saw this as a very close call, but it was not the only one they faced. Early in His ministry, Jesus returned to Nazareth and upset the people so much with His preaching that they drove Him outside of town to throw Him off a cliff. Luke 4 describes how Jesus simply walked through the angry mob and went on His way. In John 11, Jesus hears that His friend Lazarus is sick and informs His disciples that they will be going back to Judea to see Lazarus and his sisters. The disciples balk at this plan because of a safety issue.

"So when he heard that Lazarus was sick, he stayed where he was two more days, and then he said to his disciples, 'Let us go back to Judea.' 'But Rabbi,' they said, 'a short while ago the Jews there tried to stone you, and yet you are going back?' Jesus answered, 'Are there not twelve hours of daylight? Anyone who walks in the daytime will not stumble, for they see by this world's light. It is when a person walks at night that they stumble, for they have no light.'"

John 11:6-10

Jesus led His disciples right back into the face of danger. After Jesus raised Lazarus from the dead, things got even more precarious. The Jewish leaders went from wanting to kill Jesus to trying to kill Lazarus as well.

"Meanwhile a large crowd of Jews found out that Jesus was there and came, not only because of him but also to see Lazarus, whom he had raised from the dead. So the chief priests made plans to kill Lazarus as well, for on account of him many of the Jews were going over to Jesus and believing in him."

John 12:9-11

Lazarus could not help but tell the story of how Jesus had raised him from the dead. What about you? Are you willing to tell others about what Jesus has done for you? What stops you from sharing the best news the world will ever hear? What are you afraid of?

Praying for One moves us from fear to faith as we cannot help but share God's love with others. Personal safety is no longer the primary motivator for where we go and what we say. Advancing God's Kingdom takes precedence over easy living. When God captivates your heart with His salvation, He will move you into uneasy situations. Your faith will be tested, but passing the test means Ones will be saved. Do not fail by playing it safe.

THINK ABOUT IT
1. How do you feel about the reality that following Jesus might put you into a dangerous situation? How does that thought align with your beliefs about being a Christian?

2. Have you ever allowed fear to stop you from going or doing something to glorify God? What kinds of fears have you experienced in this regard?

3. Imagine facing what the first century Christians faced. They were killed for their faith. Do you know that more people are killed today for faith in Jesus than at any other point in history? Martyrdom is a present day reality. How do you feel about this?

4. How far is too far? Where does your faith end in following Jesus? What is the point where you say enough is enough and you will not follow Jesus anymore?

PRAY ABOUT IT
Ask God to help you understand what it means to be fully His. Seek to understand how following Jesus can indeed be dangerous. Commit yourself to following Jesus regardless of the cost. Pray for One and ask God to make you strong and very courageous.

NOTES:

COSTLY

If your faith costs you nothing, it is probably worthless.

Grace is free, but faith is costly.

> *"For it is by grace you have been saved, through faith—and this is not from yourselves, it is the gift of God— not by works, so that no one can boast. For we are God's handiwork, created in Christ Jesus to do good works, which God prepared in advance for us to do."*
>
> **Ephesians 2:8-10**

Salvation is a gift that is experienced through faith. Faith is defined in Hebrews 11 as "being sure of what we hope for and certain of what we cannot see." Faith compels followers of Jesus to act boldly and courageously. Faith moves us out of comfort zones and onto the front lines of advancing the gospel. Faith is what positions us to do the good works that have been prepared for us to do.

> *"In the same way, faith by itself, if it is not accompanied by action, is dead."*
>
> **James 2:17**

Faithful action is costly. Resources are required to share the gospel. Following Jesus demands that everything at our disposal be made available to Him for His purposes. Lordship says, "Nothing is mine because everything is His."

Cheap faith is what you get when you become stingy with your resources. If your money, time, or energy is not available for God to use to build His Kingdom, then the testing of your faith will reveal little to nothing of value. When God places One in your path, you will have nothing worth sharing. We are not compelled to share cheap faith because we have no confidence that it will make a difference.

This is the primary reason why the average person who claims to know Jesus as Lord and Savior will never lead another person to faith in his or her lifetime. The unwillingness of most to sacrifice produces a muddled mass of misfits. Their knowledge of Jesus separates them from this world, but their refusal to follow Him bars them from building the world to come. They are stuck in limbo claiming to cling to a faith that holds no value for today or tomorrow. It is misery at its worst. This is precisely why so many Christians exude no joy. **Cheap faith has left them empty and kept Hell full.**

WARNING: Praying for One changes this.

As your primary prayer desire moves from petty issues of self-indulgence to participating in the ultimate mission of Christ, the cost of your faith rises exponentially. God will have Ones cross your path who are needy. They will require your time when you are busy. They will need physical help when you feel your resources are diminished. They will demand energy when you are exhausted.

Ones never seem to come when it is convenient, but blessed are the interruptions. Blessed is the holy moment when God's love moves through you and moves another human to faith in Him. Blessed is the moment when miracles happen because you are generous with faith. Blessed is the moment when you realize that your faith is more precious than silver and more costly than gold. Then, and only then, will we understand the true value and power of faith in Jesus.

I pray that your entire life will be a continuous string of blessed interruptions. I pray that you enter heaven with nothing more than an army of Ones following close behind. I pray that your faith will cost you everything.

THINK ABOUT IT

1. What has your faith in Jesus cost you?

2. What are some things that you are afraid to sacrifice?

3. Realistically, where do you draw the line with generosity? How do you determine how much is too much?

4. What needs to change in your life in order for the true value of faith in Jesus to be revealed in you?

PRAY ABOUT IT

Ask God to reveal to you the value of your faith. Seek Him to discover how He wants to use you to build His Kingdom. Pray for One and begin to celebrate the interruptions.

NOTES:

CRAZY

If you are going to pray for One, you are going to have to get a little crazy. Normal patterns of thought and behavior will no longer apply. Praying for One is so transformational that you will begin to align yourself in greater and greater measure with the eternal things of God.

Friends and family will start to accuse you of taking this God thing a little too seriously. The dramatic shift in worldview that comes from praying for One will elicit discomfort in those who refuse to join in on the adventure. Scoffers scoff. It is what they do.

> *"Above all, you must understand that in the last days scoffers will come, scoffing and following their own evil desires."*

2 Peter 3:3

It is better to be out of our minds for Jesus than to follow the pattern of this world straight into oblivion. You do realize that what this world values is ultimate foolishness? People spend entire lifetimes in pursuit of things that bring no pleasure today and no hope for tomorrow. Praying for One provides purpose for today and production for tomorrow.

Escaping the ridiculous pattern of this world will appear crazy to those bound by the here and now. Your desires will change. The way you measure success will be markedly different. You will celebrate eternal victories while barely noticing the foolishness that captivates the affections of the world. Peace will reign in your heart in the midst of great turmoil. When others panic, you will be steadfast. Jesus will make you a beacon of light that draws Ones to safety out of the most turbulent seas.

The new identity that Jesus provides will set you apart. Jesus makes you holy. **Holy people are different. They do not fit into the humdrum rhythm of this world. They march to the beat of a different drummer.** The Holy Spirit is in charge and life looks different.

> *"But you are a chosen people, a royal priesthood, a holy nation, God's special possession, that you may declare the praises of him who called you out of darkness into his wonderful light. Once you were not a people, but now you are the people of God; once you had not received mercy, but now you have received mercy. Dear friends, I urge you, as foreigners and exiles, to abstain from sinful desires, which wage war against your soul."*
>
> **1 Peter 2:9-11**

Just to be clear, this is the good kind of crazy. In fact, it is the best kind of crazy. Enlightenment is a glorious thing. When your heart is beating in rhythm with God's heart, life will finally start to make sense. You will understand your purpose, calling, and reason for living. The struggle of life is not in vain but produces obvious eternal fruit.

The joy that comes from being a co-laborer with Christ is crazy good. It is contagious and compelling. The otherwise sane people of this world will experience an awakening through you. God will use you as a wakeup call for your Ones who previously have experienced life as merely a steady march toward death. Life in Christ declares that death is not the end and eternity is experienced today.

I cannot imagine that there is a way to pray for One without becoming a little crazy. It produces a crazy love for Jesus and a crazy devotion to His mission. Pack your bags. We are moving toward the lunatic fringe.

God, give us One.

THINK ABOUT IT

1. How concerned are you about what others think? How do you feel about people thinking you are over-the-top devoted to Jesus?

2. What are some ways that crazy love and devotion to Jesus should be expressed? What are the positive outcomes?

3. What are some ways that crazy love and devotion to Jesus should not be expressed? What are the negative outcomes?

4. Is there anything about your relationship with Jesus that others find a little crazy? What needs to change in your life in order for it to be crazy good?

PRAY ABOUT IT

Ask God to give you a vision of what it looks like to be fully surrendered to Him in this life. Seek Him and boldly pray that your heart would beat in rhythm with His. Pray for One and live the crazy good life

.

NOTES:

UNPREDICTABLE

When the Holy Spirit takes over, anything can happen.

Anything can happen.

Anything can happen.

Fools put limits on the Holy Spirit. The foolish choose to believe that there are certain people who cannot be saved, that there are certain places God would not ask His people to go, and that there are certain situations that are beyond God's reach. The only limits imposed on the Holy Spirit are the ones we place on Him by our stubborn refusal to yield to His leading.

Jesus described people who are born of the Spirit as being like the wind.

> *"The wind blows wherever it pleases. You hear its sound, but you cannot tell where it comes from or where it is going. So it is with everyone born of the Spirit."*
>
> **John 3:8**

How do you restrain the wind? How do you stop the wind from blowing? How do you direct which way the wind will blow?

You don't.

You do not control the wind. You just experience the wind.

In the same way, the Holy Spirit must be free to move us wherever He chooses. Every limitation we place on God carries consequences. How many Ones have not been reached because they did not fit into our preconceived notions of whom God would save? In how many places and situations was the gospel not introduced because we could not conceive of going there or being a part of that? How many times have we said "no" to God because His order simply did not fit within our narrow framework of possibilities?

Our God is the God of impossibilities! We must cease from confining Him to our ways of thinking. God's ways are higher than our ways. His thoughts are higher than our thoughts. He has perspective, power, and authority to do more than we could ever ask or imagine. It is to the impossible people, places, and situations that we must go.

If you do not do it, who will?

Nobody.

And if nobody will go, then people will not be saved.

Please allow the gravity of our calling to settle upon you. Refrain from shrugging it off. Lose the excuses, justification, and false expectations. **You are the Church. The Holy Spirit is in you. Where you go, He goes. When you speak, He speaks. When you act, He acts.**

Allow God's Spirit to blow you wherever He chooses. Miracles will happen. You can either fight against the wind or be carried by the wind. One is exhausting and futile. The other is refreshing and exhilarating. Yield to the Holy Spirit and be blown away by what God does.

Praying for One unleashes you from foolish restraints by changing your core expectation. When you pray for One, your baseline desire is to build God's Kingdom. You become unwilling to settle for less than living for things of eternal significance. You look for opportunities where previously you only saw closed doors. No person, place, or situation is beyond

God's reach because you will go anywhere anytime in order to reach anyOne.

THINK ABOUT IT

1. Describe a type of person that people would normally think is beyond God's reach. What does he/she look like, think, do, etc.?

2. What are some common limitations people put on God? How have you personally experienced this?

3. How do you feel about your personal responsibility to go, speak, and act whenever the Holy Spirit leads? What are some things He might ask you to do that would be difficult to obey?

4. You can either fight against the wind or be carried by the wind. Which would you rather and why?

PRAY ABOUT IT

Ask God to search your heart and reveal to you any limitations you have placed on His Spirit. Confess those things and repent by acknowledging that God can do anything. Pray for One and ask God to carry you on the wind of His Holy Spirit.

NOTES:

AND THEN IT GETS WEIRD

chapter nine

AND THEN IT GETS WEIRD

When did normalcy become such a popular goal?

I hear people all the time saying things like, "I just want a normal life, with a normal job, a normal family, and normal relationships."

Honestly, that seems awful. Normal is dependent on a comparison process. The only way to determine if you are normal is by comparing yourself to others. When you do this, you will find envy, coveting, competition, pride, and false views of self.

Jesus commands us to love our neighbors as we love ourselves. It is impossible to love like Jesus when normal is your primary objective. The love of Jesus is an out-of-this-world experience. That is why the Bible refers to Christians as strangers and aliens. Authentic Christ-followers are going to be weird.

Praying for One opens the door for all manner of weirdness. This prayer impacts your baseline understanding of self and positions you to navigate the pitfalls of various self-esteem issues effectively . Some people think too highly of self and are held captive by pride. Others think too lowly of self and are caught in the bondage of perpetual doubt. This is an oversimplification of the psychological issues surrounding the view of self, but the spiritual ramifications of either view result in the same ineffectiveness and purposelessness.

Unfortunately ineffectiveness and purposelessness are both pretty normal. Normal is not good.

It is impossible to obey Christ's command to love your neighbor as yourself when you do not posses a godly view of self. Praying for One connects you to the heartbeat of God and is a constant reminder that you are One. You were lost. You were separated from God. But God pursued you, saved you, and called you to participate in His mission. You have been delivered from meaningless existence into purposeful living.

With this knowledge at the forefront of your mind, you will be compelled to take action. Normal will never satisfy. You will crave weirdness. And that's when it gets really weird.

God will answer your prayers for One in the craziest ways. Your One will appear at the oddest times, in the strangest places, in the most bizarre circumstances. The supernatural cannot be explained away nor should it. Praying for One will open you up to experience the supernatural love of God flowing through you to others. There will be no doubt that God is working because no human could conceive and contrive what unfolds.

Over the last several years, I have heard many Praying for One stories. Some were touching. Some were gut-wrenching. Some were funny. Some were exciting. Each story is unique, but a common denominator in all of them is that they are weird.

Salvation is the best kind of miracle. When you pray for One, people are saved. Praying for One opens up the door for miracles. Miracles, by definition, are weird.

When I first started praying for One, I just assumed that God would answer my prayer in a normal fashion. My thoughts on evangelism were generally focused on specific attempts to take someone through a gospel presentation of some sort with an invitation to receive Christ at the end. I thought that I would pray for One and maybe invite a neighbor to church at some point, and the rest would just kind of take care of itself.

I was not prepared for the messiness of praying for One. I did not anticipate how inconvenient praying for One could be. I never considered how much time, money, and energy praying for One would cost me. And most of all, I totally underestimated the weirdness factor.

And Then You Get Puked On

One time, I met a guy at the gym named James. We were both rounding a corner in the men's locker room from different directions and almost ran into each other. He was covering his mouth with his hand and looked panicked. When I asked if he was okay, he shook his head no and then proceeded to vomit on me.

We bonded over the fact that he threw up on me, and from then on we talked whenever we saw each other at the gym. A couple of months later, I got to baptize James. It is hard to imagine that getting thrown up all over is a direct answer to prayer, but when you pray for One, it gets weird.

James started praying for One, and God introduced him to a young lady named Destiny. James is a recruiter for the Army, and Destiny was a new recruit. James knew that she was his One. He found me at the gym one day and asked me to pray with him for Destiny. James was concerned for Destiny and wanted to do everything in his power to help her know Jesus before she went off to boot camp.

James started helping Destiny train for boot camp, and this gave him the opportunity to introduce her to me at the gym. We invited her to church, and she accepted. Our church adored Destiny, and many people joined James and me in praying for her. It did not take long for Destiny to surrender her life to Christ. She was baptized one summer night at youth group, and everyone cheered like crazy!

Destiny went off to boot camp, but stays in touch with her new church family. She prays for One all the time and God has already used her greatly to share His love with others. She sent me this story about how God has answered her prayers for One.

When I shipped to basic training in the Army, I knew within ten minutes of being there that the experience was going to be a great test of my patience and faith. I have never had much patience, nor have I ever been very good at being nice to those who irritate me or those who I just don't like. I am also very quick to not like people, so you can imagine how quickly I got angry in a room full of 60 females from all different backgrounds from all over the United States.

I knew that I needed to keep my cool and not be rude to people. I decided to try to be kind to everyone, so I started praying hard. There was one female in particular who was loud, cocky, and rude, and she instantly got on my nerves. On just our second night there, she started making fun of me and acted like she owned the barracks. She was bossing everyone around. I don't know if it was the stress of the new environment, the lack of sleep, anger, or a combination of all three, but I lost my temper and went off on her. She didn't hesitate to come right back at me, and we ended up fighting.

We both received negative reports and extra duty assignments after a long lecture from the drill sergeants. I knew this type of behavior was ungodly, so I prayed for patience and help from God to make it in this new environment. I prayed for the people who were rude, obnoxious, or didn't help out in the barracks. I also continued to pray for One knowing that I could participate in God's mission even from boot camp.

All the females got split up and sent to six different companies, so I was hoping that I would be separated from the girl I had fought with. When I arrived at my training battalion, our drill sergeants had us fill out questionnaires about ourselves. They wanted to learn about our personalities and backgrounds. From behind me, I heard this one loud and obnoxious voice complaining about how dumb the questionnaire was. I turned around and saw that it was the girl I had fought with. The entire platoon got punished because of her mouth.

Not only was she in my company, she was also in my platoon. This meant that we would be together for every second of every day for the next ten weeks. Within the first few days, my hatred for her grew exponentially, but I continued to pray for her and for One.

Within the platoon, each of us was assigned a permanent battle buddy. We were not allowed to go anywhere without our battle buddies, and we were supposed to help them whenever they needed it. Teamwork with your battle buddy is essential. If you do not work well together, the drill sergeant will force you to do tons of pushups. You are also bunk and locker mates with your battle buddy, so it is pretty important that you like the person.

When our drill sergeants assigned the battle buddies, they took into consideration our personality questionnaires and tried to match us accordingly. I found myself praying not to be placed with the girl I had fought with, but while the list was being read, I asked God to put me with whomever He wanted.

You can learn a lot from your battle buddy as the two of you grow together during basic training. I really wanted to be with someone who I would enjoy getting to know. Initially, I was partnered with a really quiet girl who I did not know at all. She didn't talk much but was very neat and organized. I was very excited that my battle buddy was going to be pretty low maintenance.

In the second week of basic training, however, my battle buddy was injured and taken out of the Army. I had been praying for One every night, but I hadn't found my One yet, or so I thought. I went a few days without a battle buddy, which I liked at first, but without an assigned buddy you don't really get the opportunity to get close to anyone.

Later that week, I was one of the few people in the barracks cleaning and using my personal time when I heard someone crying in the bathroom. I went in to try to talk to whomever it was and make sure she was okay. It turned out to be the girl I hated so much. I almost just turned around and walked away, but I knew the right thing to do would be to try to comfort her.

We talked for a while, and she opened up to me about how she was so lost and that the Army was her last resort. Her family had abandoned her, and she had nothing and no one. She was completely alone, and everyone hated her because of the way she treated people. The drill sergeants got on her case a lot about it, and she was losing hope in having what it takes to get through basic training in the Army.

I can attest first hand how hard it is to go through basic training without someone by your side. I was struggling too, and I would have been ready to quit if it weren't for the people from church writing me and reminding me that Jesus was by my side. She was talking about quitting, but she didn't know where she would go or what she would do.

I continued to talk with her for quite some time, and even though she told me she wasn't really religious, she agreed to let me pray with her. After that, we started talking and praying every night. I tried to encourage her in her physical training, and my drill sergeants noticed. They decided to make her my permanent battle buddy.

That Sunday I invited her to go to church and Bible study with me. She was hesitant at first but decided to come along. She absolutely loved it and started reading my Bible every night. She asked tons of questions, and we prayed together regularly. Over the next few weeks of training, the two of us got incredibly close, and we saw amazing changes in each other.

There were the normal changes that come with boot camp. We became more disciplined, our vocabulary changed, we were more confident, and we were truly becoming soldiers. But there was more. She became much nicer, and I became more patient. We both became better Christians.

I was blessed to be a part of her baptism at the end of the cycle as she took that next step in giving her life to Jesus.

The following week was family day and graduation. I was not looking forward to either event. I knew no one was coming to see me, and I didn't want to take part in the ceremonies. She noticed I was upset, but we didn't really talk about it.

On family day, my biological dad showed up for the sole purpose of tearing me apart and embarrassing me in front of my platoon and drill sergeants. He completely put me down for everything I had worked so hard for. Fortunately, my drill sergeant took care of him and gave me a little pep talk, but I went back to the barracks instead of going out like everyone else for family day.

About an hour later, my battle buddy showed up at the barracks to comfort me and to get me to go out with her for the day. I haven't seen her since our graduation because we were sent to different places, but not a day has gone by that we have not talked to each other. We call each other every night and pray together. She is my best friend and will always be my battle buddy. I am so grateful that I continued to pray for One because God blessed me with a great friend who helps me love Jesus more.

So to sum this up…I prayed for One, got puked on, and made a friend in James. He gave his life completely to Christ and started praying for One. God answered his prayers for One by putting a young lady in his life that he suddenly felt responsible for. James went beyond the call of duty in reaching out to her and God used him to help Destiny become a Christian. Now Destiny is praying for One and her battle buddy is a Christ-follower who is also praying for One. This all occurred in less than a year!

And Then You Give Blood

I have a friend named Rebecca who loves Jesus and prays

for One. She once confided to me that she was a bit frustrated in praying for One, because her lifestyle keeps her from meeting new people. She works from home, goes to school online, and in general is pretty content with limited human interaction. All of those factors can make it a bit difficult to find someone to share God's love with each day.

Rebecca expressed that frustration to God and God answered by directing her to give blood. We were doing a blood drive at our church and Rebecca sensed a direct push from God to participate. Here is Rebecca's story in her own words.

I try to give blood regularly, but unfortunately, I pass out every time. One donation event recently took place at my church, and I went to give. As predicted, I passed out after giving blood. When I came to, I was flipped upside down on a stretcher with a nurse and three phlebotomists standing over me.

After making sure I was okay, the nurse left with instructions to the three phlebotomists to keep me talking so that I wouldn't lose consciousness again. I was feeling very nauseous and knew I could pass out again very easily.

Not knowing me, the trio asked questions about my life. I told them I was married with two daughters and what I did for a living. When I mentioned I went to church there, the trio began asking me questions about my church. That's when I felt that familiar nudge from Jesus to tell them about Him.

My first thought was, "Seriously? Now, Jesus? I may throw up on them!"

But I dove in anyway, willing to take the risk of passing out or throwing up in order to talk to them about Jesus.

The trio went on to tell me each of their own experiences in religion. All three had been exposed to religious rhetoric and doctrine but felt that their religions were missing something.

These three people understood who Jesus was in theory, but their faith was so dead that they couldn't grasp His love for them. Their own religions never talked about Jesus' love or forgiveness. They only taught condemnation and guilt. It was clear to me that none of them had a relationship with the Lord, just a strained relationship with their religion.

Then they asked me questions about my church's beliefs and services. When they compared what I told them with their experiences, they realized that what they believed was so layered in that dogma and tradition that they just assumed every church was the funeral-like experience that they were used to.

They didn't know of Jesus' joy either. It amazed me that these three people could be exposed to lifelong churchy experiences and still not know Jesus!

When they asked about specific teachings that were not biblical, my response was, "If it isn't in the Bible, then we don't teach it. We're nutty and non-denominational... both are a good thing. You should come!"

Then I gave them the service times and locations and told them where they could find me on Sunday. I even said I'd introduce them to our crazy senior pastor! I encouraged them to come and discover the love, forgiveness, and joy of Jesus, our living God, and get out of the dead-zone of religion.

We are often most effective for Jesus in our weakest moments. Rebecca was on the verge of passing out and throwing up when Jesus answered her prayer for One with three. Praying for One opens you up to being used by Jesus at anytime anywhere. Jesus gave His blood for you. What are you willing to give for Him?

And Then You Bring the Devil to Church

God often answers our prayers for One with by giving us the last person in the world we would ever think would receive His love. Praying for One moves you beyond prejudices, snap judgments, and assumptions that some people are beyond Christ's reach. God will push your comfort level and you will end up reaching people you never thought you would even speak to.

This story is from Joseph. Joseph prays for One and he serves breakfast every Saturday and Sunday in a local park to people in need. He meets all types of different people, but in this story God moved him even farther out of his comfort zone. Joseph writes:

The Lord doesn't let us pick who our One is. He tends to give us the One who puts us out of our comfort zone the most, but he always provides One.

One morning while serving breakfast to the homeless downtown, I prayed for Jesus to give me One with whom to share His love. Soon I began talking to a belligerent drunk I personally disliked. Jimmy was loud and obnoxious and routinely disrupted the message by heckling the speaker.

This morning, however, was a bit different. He was very morose, filled with self–loathing, and noticeably upset due to a fight he had with his girlfriend. While talking to him, I felt the Lord lead me to bring Jimmy to church with us after breakfast. I thought that this was just about the dumbest idea ever. There was no way I was taking a visibly drunk and loud man to church.

A little later, I found myself again talking to Jimmy about his troubles and how the Lord loves and cares for him. Again, I felt the Lord tell me to bring him to church. Again, I said no way.

As we were packing up, I realized that this was the One the Lord picked for me, and I yielded to His request. I invited Jimmy to church while secretly hoping he would reject my offer.

Jimmy shocked me when he said yes. Once I got him to finish the beer tucked inside his vest, we set off for church.

We were coming up to a traffic light when he pulled another beer out of his vest and started drinking it. I gave him the choice to stay with his beer and walk back downtown or to stay with me and go to church. He chose to stay with me instead of the beer, so I took the beer, pulled over, and threw it in the trash.

Walking into the church building was when the fun really started. Jimmy insisted on greeting people by saying, "God bless...I'm the Devil." I was a bit embarrassed and very concerned about how to get Jimmy under control. I knew that I was in way over my head and that it was inevitable that Jimmy would cause a scene.

I was acting on faith alone that Jesus knew what He was doing and that I wasn't completely deranged to bring this man to church. As the service started, he became completely engrossed in the music. Then his attention was drawn to the pastor talking about, of all things, everyone having an addiction. It was then I realized that this was the message Jesus wanted him to hear. Afterward, we spent an hour-and-a-half talking about Jesus and His great love for us. It was then that I believe the Lord began to change Jimmy's heart.

Since then Jimmy married his girlfriend, and they now have an apartment. It is the first time in more than thirteen years that he is off of the streets. Others stepped up and provided furniture, dishes, cookware, and other necessities needed to make their apartment a home. He also received the first Christmas tree and decorations in what seemed to him like forever.

The Lord also used this opportunity to teach me a lesson about judging others and thinking there are those who are too far gone to bother trying to save. I had judged Jimmy and chalked him up as another panhandling drunk who was just looking to score a free meal and a buck for another beer. Looking at Jimmy through Jesus' eyes that morning, I stopped judging, listened to his troubles, and tried showing him the love and grace Jesus shows me daily. I still find myself way outside of my comfort zone, but it is reassuring to know I am doing the work He has commanded me to do.

Jimmy still has a difficult time understanding how Jesus and "church people" can love him, but he feels God's love and thanks Him for all the things that he is receiving. He is still working on sobriety and has made many big steps toward that goal.

I am truly blessed to witness His work on my One. Taking Jimmy to church wasn't the dumbest idea after all. No one is beyond God's reach!

God loves to teach us about His love while He uses us to share His love with others. Praying for One creates a new worldview where miracles are not only possible...they are expected. Saying "no" to God gets harder and harder, because you cannot bear the thought of missing out on a pray for One opportunity.

Praying for One sets the stage for simple steps of obedience. God is always speaking, directing, and working upstream in our lives. It is easy to miss out on what God is doing when you are not tuned into His will. When the number one desire of your heart is in line with Christ's mission to seek and save the lost, your steps will sync up with the Holy Spirit and all manner of weirdness will ensue.

You will become sensitive to God's voice. When He speaks, obedience will be your first response. "Yes Lord" will be on your lips. At His direction you will smile at people, offer a kind word, and extend a gentle touch. Random act of kindness will no longer be random. You will be consistently and intentionally kind. Every appointment will be divine, because everyone is a One.

The best weirdness of all is the fruit of the Holy Spirit.

"But the fruit of the Spirit is love, joy, peace, patience, kindness, goodness, faithfulness, gentleness and self-control. Against such things there is no law. Those who belong to Christ Jesus have crucified the sinful nature with its passions and desires. Since we live by the Spirit let us keep in step with the Spirit."
Galatians 5:21-25

The normative pattern of this world is sin and selfishness. Pursuing Christ leads you into the depths of His divine nature. You will get in over your head and find yourself completely dependent on Jesus. In that beautiful place of total submission,

254

you will become available to God. You will be a resource in His hands to accomplish His will.

People will get saved, because weird works.

NORMAL

Normal?

Really? You think that normal is what you want?

Are you kidding me?

Normal is no good. Normal is joining the masses on a joyless death march. Step in line, shuffle through life, put in your time, and die. In the end, some relatives and friends can gather together, make a few clichéd remarks about your unremarkable life and then adjourn for a delicious funeral potluck. If you're lucky, someone might bring jello salad. Jello salad will be the best part of that day.

Why in the world would you pursue a normal life? People are deceived into thinking that they want to be just like everyone else. Don't you know that normal people are lost and aimless? They are going through the motions and pretending. The most exciting times in life are when a new season of their favorite show comes on. Happy, happy, joy, joy.

Really? Is that what's going to do it for you? I don't think so.

Jesus did not die for that. He came to set you free from the pattern of this world. Do not receive His grace in vain and cheapen it by wasting your life in the foolish chase to be normal. Jesus' heart breaks for the normal.

"When he saw the crowds, he had compassion on them, because they were harassed and helpless, like sheep without a shepherd. Then he said to his disciples, 'The harvest is plentiful but the workers are few. Ask the Lord of the harvest, therefore, to send out workers into his harvest field.'"
Matthew 9:36-39

The workers are few. There are not a lot of abnormal people. There are not a lot of people who live overcoming lives that produce the eternal reward of more people in the Kingdom of Heaven. Normal people just don't do that. Normal people are desperate for some crazy Christians to enter into their world to crack the façade of phony living.

If you give your life to normal, you won't matter. Life will be wasted. This is your one and only life. What are you going to do with it? We all give our lives to something. You can join the crowd and waste your most precious resource on pain avoidance, steady sailing, and the slow drift into oblivion. Or you can wake up from normal and throw yourself headlong into danger, rocked boats, and the fast track to eternity.

The choice is yours. **Normal or Jesus? Which will it be? It cannot be both. Jesus will not share you with normal, and normal will not allow you to follow Jesus.**

Praying for One produces a holy discontent. The allure of living some sort of fantasy world, Hollywood dream dissipates with every plea for One. Life has to be more than the 9-to-5, pay-the-mortgage, hustle-and-bustle struggle for who knows what. Praying for One establishes a new course. It sets a new aim. Walk on that path for a while, and it is definitely going to get weird.

Weird is good. Trust me. It is good. You have been told your whole life that weird is bad. You have probably rejected weird, made fun of weird, and done your best not to be weird. But you are weird. You are a unique individual with a personality, talents, and gifts that your Creator placed in you. He made you to be weird. Normal is just another rejection of God's authority and direction.

Buckle up. The crazy train is leaving the station. Are you on board?

THINK ABOUT IT

1. Everyone has a picture in mind about what a normal life should look like. Describe a normal life. What do you picture when you think about just living a normal life?

2. Do you struggle with the notion of being weird? Why or why not?

3. If you could make one major change in your life right now, what would it be and why?

4. How could your family, friends, neighbors, and coworkers benefit from you being weird? Do you think it is possible to be a participant in building God's Kingdom without being weird? Why or why not?

PRAY ABOUT IT

Ask God to reveal to you what you are actually living for. Are you more like a sheep without a shepherd or like one of the workers sent into the field? Ask God to give you One today to share His love with. Ask Him to deliver you from normal so that you can be sent to set the captives free.

NOTES:

DAY 32

FEAR

Fear teaches us to avoid weird and potentially dangerous situations. It is a survival mechanism that must be appropriately controlled. The decision for fight or flight is one that Christians must make on a regular basis, but we do not make that decision based on mere instinct.

Christians must listen to the Holy Spirit. Seeing God's power unleashed produces fear because it is so weird. We cannot predict, control, or contain God's power, and many avoid what's weird at all costs.

If you choose to avoid weird, you will never get to participate in God's miracles.

Miracles, by definition, are weird. God's intervention breaks the laws of nature and raises eyebrows as people take notice. When God works, miracles happen, and miracles are weird.

Weird avoidance will keep you out of God's business. **If you turn tail and run every time it gets weird, you will never understand the true wonder and beauty of following Jesus.** Think about the first disciples. They experienced some truly weird stuff, and there were times that it freaked them out.

> "That day when evening came, he said to his disciples, 'Let us go over to the other side.' Leaving the crowd behind, they took him along, just as he was, in the boat. There were also other boats with him. A furious squall came up, and the waves broke over the boat, so that it was nearly swamped. Jesus was in the stern, sleeping on a cushion. The disciples woke him and said to him, 'Teacher, don't you care if we drown?'
> "He got up, rebuked the wind and said to the waves, 'Quiet!

Be still!' Then the wind died down and it was completely calm.

"He said to his disciples, 'Why are you so afraid? Do you still have no faith?'

"They were terrified and asked each other, 'Who is this? Even the wind and the waves obey him!'"

Mark 4:35-41

Following Jesus is not for the faint of heart. There are going to be times when you cry out to Him, "Don't you care if we drown?" You will end up in some pretty crazy situations with Jesus. Your boat is going to get rocked by furious waves. Water will be pouring in. You will be in a panic, but where is Jesus? Is He not concerned? Is He not going to do anything?

You will pray something like this: "Look, God, we are drowning down here. We are taking on water, and this boat is going to sink. You sent us out here into this dangerous situation, but you do not seem the least bit concerned. Do something!"

And God will act. And it is going to be weird.

The disciples went from being afraid of the waves to being terrified of God's power.

Fear is what prevents people from experiencing God's power. The fear of the unknown and the intense realization of who God is prove to be more than many are willing to endure. They run for the hills at the slightest sense of ensuing weirdness.

This is your warning. Praying for One makes things weird. You will see God do things you never imagined possible. He will put you into situations that no rational human being would willingly walk into. His authority will break through the natural realm, and miracles will occur in you, around you, and through you.

Be afraid. Oh, yes, be very afraid. Just make sure that it is Almighty God you fear and nothing else. He is the only One worthy of your fear, and true fear of God compels you to love, trust, and follow Him. Fear of the Lord is the beginning of wisdom. It is a reverent, healthy fear that reminds us that we have nothing to fear.

THINK ABOUT IT

1. What are you afraid of? Make a list things and situations that produce fear in you.

2. Why are you afraid? What purpose does fear serve?

3. Does fear control you, or does God's Spirit in you control fear? Do you make decisions from a position of fear about potential outcomes or from a place of trust and obedience to God's authority?

4. Have you ever felt like the disciples did in that boat? Describe a time when you were truly freaked out and wondered if God would save you. Does it make more sense to fear the waves or the God who controls the waves?

PRAY ABOUT IT

Confess your fears to God. Be honest about what you are afraid of. Ask God to help you to overcome fear by trusting in Him. Commit to following the Holy Spirit with the knowledge that it is going to get weird.

NOTES:

WEIRDER

Praying for One is weird, but why not make it weirder?

I totally understand how embracing weirdness completely flies in the face of our civilized sensibilities. After all, we do not want to make anyone uncomfortable. We do not want to ruffle any feathers or cause people to get the wrong idea. The world we live in tells us that it is okay to discuss anything except the one thing that actually matters.

Christianity is a weird thing in a world where everything is right except for the one thing that makes an exclusive claim. Our society pushes the belief that all beliefs are valid as long as they do not infringe on any other beliefs. So, proclaiming that Jesus is the only way to Heaven is going to be increasingly weird and is probably going to get you into trouble.

There are a few different ways to respond to the cultural rejection of Jesus as absolute truth.

Some people become angry, fearful Christians who defend the faith with a great deal of zeal, but little compassion, empathy, or grace. Others become timid Christians who refuse to offend anyone and try to mix their Jesus with a spoonful of pop culture nonsense in hopes that some of the medicine will go down.

But there is another way…a weirder way.

You could just share the truth in love.

Can that work? Absolutely!

But you must understand where people are coming from. Acknowledge that proclaiming absolute truth in a relative truth kind of world is weird. Prepare yourself to deal with people who will have their worldviews cave in around them as they come into contact with the reality of Jesus. Jesus disturbs and shakes people to the core. They may be frustrated, argumentative, grief-stricken, distraught, and/or afraid.

In the weirdness of that moment, go ahead and make it weirder by being like Jesus.

In John 4, Jesus has a weird encounter with a Samaritan woman at a well. The whole thing was strange from the start. Jesus asked her for a drink and she responded in an argumentative fashion. Her first response was to point out that Jesus was a Jew and she was a Samaritan. Jews and Samaritans did not associate. This was weird, but Jesus made it weirder by telling her that she should ask Him for living water. Their encounter continued moving from weird to weirder as Jesus made her increasingly uncomfortable until He revealed Himself as the Messiah to her.

> *"The woman said, 'I know that Messiah' (called Christ) 'is coming. When he comes, he will explain everything to us.' Then Jesus declared, 'I, the one speaking to you—I am he.'"*
> **John 4:25-26**

This truth completely changed the Samaritan woman's life. She returned to her village and told everyone to come and see the Messiah, and they all believed. You do not know how powerful a weird encounter getting weirder can be. **Those weird moments are often holy moments that need to be embraced. Do not run away or shut it down. Press into the moment and let the weird get weirder.**

Heaven grows exponentially in some of the weirdest ways.

THINK ABOUT IT

1. What is the weirdest conversation you have ever had about Jesus?

2. How did you feel while having that conversation?

3. What are you inclined to do when things get weird? Are you more likely to let it get weirder or do you try to move it out of the realm of weird?

4. Are you afraid of being labeled as a "crazy Jesus freak"? Why or why not? Can you be weird without coming across as totally insane and unrelatable? What would that look like?

PRAY ABOUT IT

Ask God to help you recognize holy moments where getting weirder is the thing to do. Pray for courage to move out of your comfort zone. Pray for One and expect that God will position you to share His love with others in some pretty weird ways.

NOTES:

A TALE
OF TWO
KINGDOMS

chapter ten

A TALE OF TWO KINGDOMS

Every day you are faced with a critical choice. Whose kingdom will you build?

Your life will be spent on one of two pursuits. You will either live to build your personal kingdom, or you will live to build Christ's eternal Kingdom.

If you long to build Christ's Kingdom, you must make this choice each and every day. The universal reality of sin and the fallen nature of humanity set our default choice to personal kingdom building. The prevailing attitudes of our culture all center on selfishness, greed, and self-glorification. Failing to build Christ's Kingdom intentionally will lead automatically to the secondary pursuit of looking out for #1.

Our world constantly projects the self-serving message, "Look out for #1."

If we do not actively submit to Jesus and His mission, we easily slip back into the nature of sin and selfishness. The beauty of praying for One is that it causes us to actively choose to participate in building Christ's Kingdom.

The phrase "Look out for #1" takes on a whole new meaning for followers of Jesus. We are blissfully aware that each One is one more person Jesus died for. Each One is one more for the Kingdom of Heaven. We are always on the lookout for #1, but the focus is decidedly off of self and is fixed on finding One more for Jesus.

When you pray for One, you make the conscious choice to build Christ's Kingdom. If you fail to make this choice, your life will go into default mode, and you will build a worthless, temporary kingdom for self. It is important to take an inventory of your life regularly. Ask the Lord to search your heart and reveal what you are living for. Dig deep and examine your baseline motivations.

What drives you? What compels you to action? What excites you? What stories do you long to tell? What is your predominant prayer?

One of the best diagnostic questions to ask is, "Am I available to the Lord?"

There is a strong temptation to compartmentalize our lives. We set aside specific times that we are available to serve Jesus. If Jesus calls us to action during what we have deemed to be "His" time, then we jump at the opportunity and faithfully serve. But if He calls during a predetermined break, then He's going to have to wait. The problem is that Jesus does not wait, and if we refuse to do His work, the task will go undone.

Constant availability is a foundational principle for following Christ. When He says, "Go," we go. When He says, "Speak," we speak. When He says, "Jump," we do not waste time on silly questions like "How high?" We just jump and depend on Jesus to do the rest.

I pray for One every day, but that doesn't mean that I am always available to the Lord. I often find myself compartmentalizing my life into time that I am available to God and times that I am not. It is kind of like putting a "do not disturb" sign on a hotel room door. If I am not exceptionally careful, I will sequester myself from God. I shut Him out at certain times and make myself off-limits to Him.

God is not cool with my unavailability. In fact, He often answers my prayers for One when I am huddled in my private space with the deadbolt turned, the chain securely fastened, and the "do not disturb" sign in place. When I retreat into my personal world, the Lord stands at the door and knocks. It turns out that Jesus is not a fan of restricted areas. When He becomes your Lord, Jesus is given an all-access pass to every element of your life. Close a door on Him, and He will knock. And knock. And knock.

We must choose to maintain an open-door policy. It will not happen by accident. Again, the default mode is to hide away and build a private kingdom based on self. We must make conscious decisions to build Christ's Kingdom instead of our own. Praying for One works as a doorstop to keep your life open to the work of seeking and saving the lost. Praying for One puts you at the ready for when Jesus calls. The risk of compartmentalization is reduced tremendously because there is no such thing as "me-time." There is only "Jesus-time."

I enjoy working out. I go to the gym each weekday morning. It is part of my regular rhythm and routine. I look forward to my time at the gym because I put my headphones on and zone out from the rest of the world for a while. My workouts are an important part of my relationship with God, but if I am not careful, I can miss opportunities to share His love with others.

Personally, I blame the mirrors.

There are just too many mirrors at the gym. Everywhere I look, there are mirrors, and in each mirror, I see me. So often, when I am working out, my perspective changes. Instead of looking at everyone through the lens of praying for One and with a godly perspective, I see them only through the lens of self. Of course, that is if I see them at all. Sometimes I am so fixated on the image in those blasted mirrors that I see nothing but me.

When I am not careful, the gym becomes the dreaded "me-time." I wonder how many Ones I have missed sharing the love of Jesus with because I was unavailable. When I slip into the default mode of personal kingdom-building, I find myself completely unaware of what I am missing out on.

I recently found myself engaged in the battle to determine which kingdom to build while at the gym. I was pretty excited because all through my workout I prayed for One. I smiled at people. I said, "Hi." I was on alert for any opening to share the love of Jesus. I looked at every person like they could be the One.

One of the neat benefits of praying for One is that God will remove prejudices from your heart. Over the years, Jesus has worked to deliver me from all kinds of prejudicial thinking. Since anyone could be the One, God has revealed how crucial it is to put aside preconceived judgments and discriminatory fears. Things like race, age, social status, and economic position can become roadblocks to sharing Christ with others.

I would love to declare that I am prejudice-free, but there are still certain people who I refuse to share the love of Jesus with. And of course, one of them walked into the gym that day.

I had just finished my workout and was grabbing one last drink at the water fountain when I looked up and saw him. Okay, I did not actually see him. What I saw was his hideous t-shirt. It was this disgusting burnt orange color with a white longhorn across the chest. He was wearing a University of Texas shirt.

Most people could probably get over this man's poor choice of clothing, but I am a graduate of Texas A&M University, and Aggies do not like Longhorns. It just isn't natural. The two universities are rivals, and as a graduate of A&M, I will admit that we Aggies may have a bit of inferiority complex. Over the years, the Longhorns have flooded the great state of Texas with their burnt orange paraphernalia. For some bizarre reason, the masses have been duped into thinking that they look good in that ridiculous color.

One of the benefits of living in New Hampshire is that I am over 2,000 miles away from the University of Texas. When you live in Texas, your eyes kind of adjust to the constant barrage of burnt orange you are forced to behold on a daily basis. The standard joke is that, if you see someone wearing a Texas A&M shirt, you know that the person probably went to school at A&M, but if you see someone wearing a Longhorns shirt, the person probably went to Wal-Mart. Having lived in New Hampshire for a couple of years caused me to forget about my prejudices toward Longhorn fans because I rarely encounter them this far north.

So when I looked up and saw that t-shirt, I was in a little bit of shock. It was so utterly out of place, and I was perplexed as to why someone in New Hampshire would wear it. Did this man lose a bet? Was he vision-impaired and being victimized by a cruel caretaker? Had he received this shirt as a gag gift and felt obligated to wear it in public? Could he possibly be from Texas and actually like the Longhorns?

As I pondered the possibilities, I felt a familiar urge. It was the Holy Spirit-driven, pray for One urge. I was supposed to share God's love with the guy in the Longhorns shirt. I had never seen this man before, but the shirt provided an easy way to begin a conversation. All I needed to do was ask him why a guy in New Hampshire was wearing a shirt from Texas.

I easily envisioned the entire conversation. I would tell him that I was from Texas and then make a little joke about the Longhorns. He would chuckle and ask what brought me to New Hampshire. I would respond by telling him that I am a pastor of church in the area. He would ask which one. I would tell him how amazing our church is and then invite him. He would say that he would love to come because he has never been to a church before. I would find out his name and from then on greet him by name and remind him about the invitation to come to church. I would pray for him everyday and begin to have meaningful conversations whenever I saw him at the gym. I would find out about his family, his job, his struggles, and so on. We would become friends, and I would introduce him to Jesus.

I could see the whole scenario, but in that moment, I froze. When I looked up from the water fountain no words came out of my mouth. The man just walked by me and into the locker room. I stood there for a few seconds and realized that I had missed a pray for One opportunity. I felt pretty crummy about not responding to God's leading, so I started to rationalize the whole thing away. I thought about how weird it would have been to start a conversation with someone about how much I hated his wardrobe choice. I convinced myself that he was not really my One for that day and that God would provide someone else.

With that frame of mind, I went into the locker room to shower. During my shower, I prayed. As I prayed, God made it clear that I had been disobedient. I told God I was sorry for not talking to the guy. I asked God to give me another chance. I prayed for One.

When I came out of the shower and rounded the corner toward my locker, guess who I ran into? That's right...Longhorn t-shirt guy. I actually bumped into him, but the only words that came out my mouth were "excuse me." He muttered something back and continued on his way. Again I felt the Holy Spirit urge me to speak to this guy, but I did not do it. I watched him walk away for the second time, and I knew that I had blown it again.

I started to chase him down, but all I had on was a towel. I completely psyched myself out as I thought about trying to share the love of Jesus with a complete stranger while I was half naked. I hung my head in disappointment and went to my locker to get dressed. I continued to pray while I put my clothes on. I told God that I was sorry and that I would get the next One. I promised God that I would be bolder and more obedient.

As I walked out of the locker room to head to my car, I was reading an email on my phone. My eyes were down, and if Longhorn t-shirt guy had not physically bumped into me, I would not have seen him at all. I looked up from my phone and was shocked to have a third opportunity to start a conversation with the guy. This time, he said, "Excuse me," and I muttered something back. He gave me this strange look of recognition like he was waiting to have a conversation since it was the third time we had run into each other in a thirty-minute period.

When I looked back down at my phone, he kind of shrugged his shoulders and walked away. I took three steps forward and froze. I stood still and prayed. I could not believe that I had blown three pray for One opportunities with the same guy in less than thirty minutes. I am not sure how long I stood there contemplating my next move.

Finally, I decided to go back into the locker room to talk to him. There was just one problem…I had no idea what he looked like. I had not actually looked at his face. I did not know his height, hair color, or even ethnicity. All I had seen was that burnt orange t-shirt.

When I went back into the locker room, there was not a burnt orange t-shirt in sight. He had changed clothes, and I had no way of identifying him. I received some pretty awkward stares as I walked through the locker room looking everybody over. I looked, but I could not find the guy.

I failed. Seriously…I failed. There is no happy ending to this story. I did not find the guy the next day or the day after that. I did not see that same t-shirt a month later. There was never a conversation, an invitation to church, or a gospel presentation. I had a chance, and I missed it.

I failed because I allowed a prejudice to slip me back into the default mode of personal kingdom-building. I talk to people all the time who, for some reason, cannot handle the notion of failure. They like to say things like, "Failure is not an option."

Failure is always an option.

Praying for One does not guarantee success. God will answer the prayer. He will make you aware of opportunities. God will place an intense love for the lost deep in your heart, put people who do not know Him yet directly in your path, and nudge you to share His love with them. But you must make a choice. Which kingdom will you build?

I find this to be the most troubling part of God's plan. I do not want failure to be an option, but He chose me to be His ambassador, and I am painfully aware of my many shortcomings. On one hand it is an honor to know the Master's business and to have meaningful purpose, but on the other hand I am disturbed by the reality of the mission. If I do not do what God has called me to do, then it does not get done.

The gravity of this truth is essential to grasp. Failure is always an option. If we refuse to recognize this reality, we end up living in a land of make believe. We will explain away failure and make up little scenarios in hopes of finding comfort.

In the case of Longhorn t-shirt guy, I could easily placate myself by thinking, "God will send someone else," or "God was just trying to teach me a lesson." I can pretend that I did not fail because God got my attention and I learned something.

But I did fail. I prayed for One. God provided One. I failed to act.

Praying for One is about more people in the Kingdom of Heaven. We will never accidently fall into building Christ's Kingdom. We must intentionally choose to do it.

Recognizing and owning failure is important, because it causes us to deal with the grief, guilt, shame, and remorse that accompanies sin. When we pretend that we do not fail or that it does not matter if we fail, then sin is readily accepted and the default choice of personal kingdom building is made. Knowing that failure is always an option keeps us at the ready and primes us to choose to build Christ's Kingdom.

Your life is a tale of two kingdoms. In the end, only one kingdom will remain. Make the choice to build the Kingdom of Heaven.

#1

My son came home from elementary school one day and announced that he was the fastest person in his school. At first, I was impressed and congratulated him, but then I began to wonder how it was determined that he was the fastest. So I asked him some questions.

"Ace, so you are telling me that you are the fastest person in your school. Is that right?"

"Yes, Dad."

"Okay. Did you have a race at school today?"

"Yep."

"Was the race with the entire school?"

"Well, no. It was just my class."

"Oh, so you raced everyone in your class?"

"No, just the boys."

"Okay, so you raced all the boys in your class?"

"Not all the boys. There were five of us."

"So you beat four other boys from your class in a race today?"

"No. I came in third, but I'm the fastest!"

I found the interaction amusing because I knew that my son was not intending to lie or exaggerate. He simply had a distorted view of reality. He had convinced himself that being in third place out of a small group of boys was the same thing as being in first place out of the entire school. I could have chalked it up to childish foolishness, but then I realized that as adults we do the same thing.

We say things like, "God is #1 in my life. God is in first place. He is Lord."

We say these things because we want them to be true. We convince ourselves that they are true, but we do not ask the tough questions to determine what is actually real. **It is easy to declare that God is #1, but what if we allowed our Heavenly Father to ask some questions?** That exchange might go like this.

"Child of mine, you are telling me that I am #1 in your life. Is that right?"

"Yes, Father."

"Oh good. So, since I am #1, does that mean that you have time to spend with me today?"

"Well, no God. I am very busy today. There is a lot on my agenda. I'm under a ton of pressure. Today is just not good for me, but you are still #1."

"So, since I am #1, does that mean that you have energy to serve me with today?"

"Well, no God. I am exhausted today. You know that I haven't been feeling well, and I have just had so much to do. I really need some me-time just to relax for a bit. I will serve you when I am feeling at my best, but don't wait around on me. You go ahead and do what you do without me."

"So, since I am #1, does that mean that you have money to invest in my eternal Kingdom?"

"Hey…hold on there a minute, Big Guy. I thought we agreed that money was off the table. You are #1, but this is my money!"

"So, in reality, I am not #1 in your life. You have placed many things ahead of me and convinced yourself otherwise."

Crickets.

> *"But seek first his kingdom and his righteousness, and all these things will be given to you as well."*
> **Matthew 6:33**

THINK ABOUT IT

1. Make a list of things that people put ahead of God.

2. Look at the list you made and circle the three that you struggle with the most. Why do you struggle with these? Write a sentence or two about why you allow each of these things to usurp God's ultimate authority.

3. What specific changes do you need to make today in order for God to be authentically #1 in your life?

4. What safeguards do you need to have in your life to ensure that tomorrow you will not revert back to some form of personal kingdom building where God is not #1?

PRAY ABOUT IT

Pray for One because when your ultimate desire is to build God's Kingdom, He is #1. Ask God to use you to build His Kingdom. Search your heart and confess any areas where God is not #1.

NOTES:

ALL-ACCESS

There are two kingdoms. There is your kingdom, and there is God's Kingdom.

Jesus is Lord, but He is not Lord over your kingdom. He is Lord over His Kingdom. This is a crucial distinction to make.

Simply thinking that Jesus will be Lord over "my" life can produce a number of potential problems. This common phrase can set expectations that are totally inaccurate. If I believe that Jesus is Lord over "my" life, then I am tempted to assume that He will always act and lead in my best interests.

Like right now, you may be thinking: "Well, of course. God always leads and works in my best interests."

What in the world ever made you think that? It simply is not true.

God leads and acts in His best interests. He is working to build His eternal Kingdom, not your earthly kingdom. He will wreck your earthly kingdom in a heartbeat if it means adding to His eternal Kingdom.

Disturbing? Absolutely!

Bad theology has set most of us up for failure and extreme disappointment.

The manner in which most Christians pray is pretty revealing. Our prayers generally center on some element of earthly kingdom building. We pray things like, make me happy, keep me well, protect my family, increase my comfort, relieve my suffering, prevent my failure, fix my mistakes, and so forth.

Prayer becomes about all me, all the time.

Jesus is Lord. Period. He is Lord. He is Lord over all. There will be nothing that is not under His authority.

> *"Therefore God exalted him to the highest place and gave him the name that is above every name, that at the name of Jesus every knee should bow, in heaven and on earth and under the earth, and every tongue acknowledge that Jesus Christ is Lord, to the glory of God the Father."*
> **Philippians 2:9-11**

Jesus' Kingdom is the only thing that matters because it is the only thing that will remain. Why in the world would we waste energy, time, and prayer on building our own earthly kingdoms? Jesus is not Lord over my kingdom. He does not exist to serve my every whim. He is not some genie in a bottle who, if I rub Him just the right way, will do my bidding.

Remaking Jesus into the lord we want is the sickest form of idolatry possible. We do not convince Jesus to do our will. We do not change His mind to align with our desires. We are transformed by His Lordship. He remakes us in His image. We are born again into His eternal life. This world and its desires will all pass away. Do not waste another prayer on the extreme foolishness of personal kingdom building. Too much is at stake to play that game.

You are a chosen child of God, and you were bought at a price. Jesus gave His life for you. He took your sin upon Himself and put it to death on the cross. You are set apart for holy purposes.

Lordship requires full access to every corner of who you are. When you receive salvation and accept that Jesus is Lord, you grant Him an all-access pass. Nothing is off-limits. No doors are closed. There are no dark corners to hide away in. His light permeates through your entire being, and you are completely transformed.

Fighting His Lordship is ultimate misery. Jesus stands at the door of your heart and knocks. Don't just crack it open to take a peek. Rip that door off the hinges, chop it into little pieces, burn it, and scatter the ashes in every direction. Praying for One does this. It acknowledges that you are all His, all the time. When the primary prayer desire is to build His Kingdom, all-access is guaranteed.

THINK ABOUT IT

1. Think about how you typically pray. Do your prayers follow a pattern? If so, what does the pattern consist of? Are there things you pray for every day?

2. What percentage of your time in prayer is spent seeking God's will verses asking God to do your will?

3. What do you think about the idea that God would wreck your kingdom to build His eternal Kingdom? What could that look like?

4. Can you say with confidence that God has an all-access pass to your life? Is there anything that is off-limits? Why or why not?

PRAY ABOUT IT

Acknowledge that Jesus is Lord. He is Lord over all. Commit yourself to build His Kingdom. Ask Him to reveal anything in you that you have made off-limits to Him. Open yourself fully to Jesus and give Him an all-access pass.

NOTES:

FAILURE

It drives me nuts when people say that failure is not an option.

Failure is always an option.

It is a terrible option that should be avoided, but it is an option nonetheless.

It is important to deal with the reality that we could fail to do what God asks us to do. If not, we are left to make excuses, redefine success, or simply never try to do anything significant for the Kingdom of Heaven.

Ultimate victory is secured through Jesus, but there are daily battles to be fought, and they matter. Doing the good we ought to do matters. Seeking and saving the lost matters. Sharing God's love matters. Praying for One matters.

Far too much Christian teaching focuses on the personal benefits of following Jesus. People are taught that they will have better marriages, happier families, more success at work, stronger reputations, and healthier relationships if they just do a little more work for Jesus. I have personally encountered hundreds of people who have heard that messaging and responded by saying, "Thanks, but no thanks."

There is this look about them that communicates, "I'm good." I'm good where I am. I'm good with a less-than-stellar marriage. I'm good being a mediocre parent. I'm good putting in minimal effort at my job. I'm good with my sketchy reputation. I'm good with my toxic relationships. I'm good.

They aren't good, and they just don't care. Apathy rules the day, and unless the motivation is higher than some better version of self, they aren't interested.

Praying for One provides new motivation. When your predominant prayer desire is to share God's love so that there will be more people in the Kingdom of Heaven, you become inspired to follow hard after Jesus. The stakes are high and failure will cost far more than some temporary discomfort. If you do not share Jesus with your family, friends, neighbors, and coworkers, there is a good chance that nobody will.

Failure is real, and the consequences are eternal.

How is that for a kick in the rear?

> *"Examine yourselves to see whether you are in the faith; test yourselves. Do you not realize that Christ Jesus is in you—unless, of course, you fail the test?"*
> **2 Corinthians 13:5**

Anytime we fail to do the good we ought to do, we sin. There are consequences to sin. We are called to bring life into the world through our obedience to Jesus and through carrying out His mission to seek and save the lost. Failure to do this means that people will not know. They will continue in death.

I implore you to give yourself fully to the work Jesus calls His Church to do.

If you fail, learn and grow from it so that you will be less likely to fail again. Refrain from making excuses, redefining success, or not trying. Confess your failures. Repent of your mistakes. Allow Jesus to pick you up and put you back in the game.

Pray for One and go get One.

THINK ABOUT IT

1. Remember a time when you failed to do something God wanted you to do. What were the circumstances and the situation?

2. How did you deal with the failure? Did you own it and grow from it, or did you blow it off by making excuses?

3. What consequences came about because of your failure? What are some possible consequences that could have happened?

4. Does making the connection between obeying Jesus and how it impacts others motivate you to be more faithful? Why or why not?

PRAY ABOUT IT

Confess your failure to God. Repent by asking Him to change how you think about the consequences of disobedience. Ask God to remind you of what is truly at stake and the eternal nature of what hangs in the balance.

NOTES:

INTENTIONAL

Purposeful action begins with intent.

The human default mode is personal kingdom building. Left to our own devices and sin natures, we will always build temporary kingdoms that are based on personal preferences and desires. Since we are earthbound in our thinking, we cannot escape our primal instincts without receiving a higher perspective.

God sees what we cannot. He knows what we do not. His ways are different and His Kingdom is better.

> *"For my thoughts are not your thoughts, neither are your ways my ways,' declares the LORD.*
> *"As the heavens are higher than the earth, so are my ways higher than your ways and my thoughts than your thoughts.'"*
> **Isaiah 55:8-9**

Transformational thinking is required for participation in building God's Kingdom. No one accidently falls into the eternal Kingdom-building business. It is not the kind of thing that just sort of happens as you go along. It is not the normal course, so intentionality is required.

Praying for One is a thought-transforming juggernaut. When we pray for One, we recognize that our core identity and purpose are found in the eternal things of God. Responsibility is accepted for the calling at hand. Intent is clearly established as we seek God's best instead of the temporary insanity found in creating a fleeting kingdom of worthless junk.

Praying for One sets our feet on the straight and narrow path. Our vision is aligned with who Jesus is, and the standard confusion that swirls around the meaning of life is squashed underfoot with every intent-filled stride. Proper intent makes once-powerful distractions impotent. Things that previously pulled our heartstrings and led us astray have no power over us when our primary focus is more people in the Kingdom of Heaven.

The goal is more people in the Kingdom of Heaven.

Do not forget, forsake, or dismiss the mission of Jesus. Nothing destroys Kingdom-building intent faster than simply rejecting Christ's mission. If you do not remain intently focused on seeking and saving the lost, you will revert to some form of foolishness. You will build worthless relationships that do not reveal Jesus or lead people into relationships with Him. You will build a lifestyle that reflects what you value most and holds no value for eternity. You will build a legacy of regret that will crumble in ruins until no sign of what you built remains.

Jesus has gone to prepare a place in His Father's house for everyOne. He is building, and there is room. Our job is to invite others to dwell in His heavenly home. Expect that God will use you. Pray for One and set forth with the intent that today will not be lived in vain.

Heaven does not notice when your personal kingdom grows. It has no regards for your possessions, portfolio, or plans. Heaven could care less if you enjoy all the success this world has to offer. Heaven knows it does not matter.

But Heaven erupts in praise every time a lost One is found.

"In the same way, I tell you, there is rejoicing in the presence of the angels of God over one sinner who repents."
Luke 15:10

THINK ABOUT IT

1. How does intent impact actions? Think about yesterday. What did you intend to do? Where you purposeful in your intentions, or did you merely go through the motions?

2. If you are not intentional with your purpose, what will an average day look like for you? What will you accomplish? What will be the end result?

3. Evaluate your life. What are your intentions in your relationships, work, leisure, and so forth?

4. Are you building your kingdom or God's Kingdom? How do you know?

PRAY ABOUT IT

Ask God to search your heart and to reveal any intentions you hold onto that are not from Him. Pray for One and seek God's best by committing yourself to building His eternal Kingdom.

NOTES:

I TRIPLE DOG DARE YOU

chapter eleven

I TRIPLE DOG DARE YOU

I love Easter.

I'm not putting it on par with Christmas, but I do love it.

Christmas is my number one holiday for obvious reasons... presents. On the holiday celebration scale, Easter is below Christmas for the simple fact that the gift giving and receiving aspect is far less substantial. In that regard, Easter cannot really compete with Christmas.

However, if you took Christmas out of the equation, then Easter would be my favorite.

Easter is a special time of celebration for many reasons. The resurrection of Jesus is the single greatest thing to ever happen on planet earth. Easter commemorates that event as families gather together, go to church, and enjoy a delicious, home-cooked meal. Easter marks the end of winter and the beginning of spring. It reminds us of new life and how all that was dead can be revived.

Everything about Easter is great, but my favorite part is the Easter baskets. Easter mornings brought great excitement as I woke up early to search for my basket. I have amazing memories of digging through fake grass to find every last morsel of candy.

Inside plastic eggs, there were jellybeans, gumdrops, marshmallow chicks, egg-shaped chocolates with crunchy malted centers, and foil-wrapped chocolate eggs with sweetly delicious insides that looked like yolks. The plastic eggs formed a perimeter of sorts surrounding the centerpiece of the basket. It was as if the eggs were bowing down before the piece de resistance of all Easter candy...the Chocolate Easter Bunny.

I mean the solid chocolate Easter Bunny, not the cheap hollow version. A solid chocolate Easter Bunny can last a kid for weeks if it is eaten correctly. A well-placed nibble here and there has actually been known to stretch Easter all the way into May for some disciplined children. Employ the right strategy on solid chocolate Easter bunny eating, and you have a gift that keeps on giving.

On one particular Easter morning, I woke up and went in search of my Easter basket. I was at a transitional age where my Mom and Dad wanted to move me from the frivolity of youth into a deeper understanding of the meaning of Easter. While I appreciate their intent, their methodology left much to be desired.

I found my Easter basket, but there were no delicious candy treats nestled inside. The fake grass concealed nothing of value.

The only candy I found was an old and cracked white jellybean that had gotten lodged in the wicker on the bottom of the basket left over from some Easter past. It tasted like a stale, semisweet, chewy communion cracker.

Instead of candy, my Easter basket contained an assortment of flower seeds and gardening tools. These are not the things that adolescent boys dream of. I made my disappointment clear. Easter was ruined.

I spent the remainder of the day pouting. My Mom and older sister went outside in the afternoon to plant a flower garden. They invited me to join them, but I refused. They took my sister's seeds and carefully planted them in the backyard, but I just threw my seeds on a shelf in my room. In the weeks that followed, every time I saw those seeds in my room, I got angry. I did not want seeds. I wanted candy. Those seeds sat on a shelf collecting dust and causing me angst.

One afternoon, my Mom and sister came through the house looking for the camera. They were both clearly excited about something in the backyard. I went outside with them to see what all the commotion was about. The flowers had bloomed. I took a few photos of them in front of their beautiful flower garden and I realized that I had totally missed out on something good.

I did not have a garden. All I had were seeds on a shelf.

Sadly, this is the experience that many who claim to follow Christ will have when they come to the end of their lives. They will look back at their years hoping to see a flower garden, but there will be only seeds on a shelf.

Seeds are only good if they are sown. Jesus calls us to participate in His mission of seeking and saving the lost, but for many, the transition from merely receiving grace to giving grace never occurs. One of the best things about following Jesus is that we are not just recipients of His Kingdom; we are participants in building His Kingdom. Jesus entrusts His mission to us and goes with us to plant, cultivate, and harvest.

Christ's words are clear in this regard:

"Then Jesus came to them and said, 'All authority in heaven and on earth has been given to me. Therefore go and make disciples of all nations, baptizing them in the name of the Father and of the Son and of the Holy Spirit, and teaching them to obey everything I have commanded you. And surely I am with you always, to the very end of the age.'"
Matthew 28:18-20

There is a point very early in your relationship with Jesus when it is crucial to move beyond every "what will I get out of this" kind of thinking. The focus must move from the frivolity of self to the seriousness of Christ's mission. We receive the gift of salvation and then we receive the gift of seeds.

God's desire is that none would perish.

"The Lord is not slow in keeping his promise, as some understand slowness. He is patient with you, not wanting anyone to perish, but everyone to come to repentance."
2 Peter 3:9

God's will cannot be done if we keep our seeds on a shelf. Life is a meaningless void of nothingness apart from the mission of Jesus. We have the amazing opportunity to celebrate Easter every day. When we plant seeds by sharing Christ with others, we get to be eyewitnesses to the resurrection of Christ within new believers!

Praying for One sets the stage for a huge harvest. Every day is about planting seeds. Each conversation cultivates the soil.

Seeds are taken off the shelf and scattered liberally. God's grace is limitless, so we never run out of seeds. There is never a need to be stingy with the gospel. When you follow Jesus, you want what He wants, and He wants a huge harvest.

> *"Remember this: Whoever sows sparingly will also reap sparingly, and whoever sows generously will also reap generously. Each man should give what he has decided in his heart to give, not reluctantly or under compulsion, for God loves a cheerful giver. And God is able to make all grace abound to you, so that in all things at all times, having all that you need, you will abound in every good work. As it is written:*
> *'He has scattered abroad his gifts to the poor; his righteousness endures forever.'*
> *Now he who supplies seed to the sower and bread for food will also supply and increase your store of seed and will enlarge the harvest of your righteousness. You will be made rich in every way so that you can be generous on every occasion, and through us your generosity will result in thanksgiving to God."*
>
> **2 Corinthians 9:6-11**

What will the end result of your life be? If it does not result in thanksgiving to God, then it will be wasted. The simple fact that you are still breathing means that you are here for a purpose. God wants to use you so that there will be more people in the Kingdom of Heaven.

Can it really be this simple? Can praying for One actually work in your life?

You will never know if you do not try it.

Many people have decided that evangelism is not for them. Some believe that this type of activity is just for the religiously trained.

Others are paralyzed by the fear of rejection. There are those who "tried it once" and had some form of a negative experience. Some worry about how others will perceive them. They do not want to be viewed as pushy, hyper-religious, judgmental, or Jesus-freaky.

Praying for One destroys the excuses because, when you pray for One, God changes your heart. His love drives out fear. His mercy removes prejudices. His mission replaces concern for self.

So, why not pray for One? What do you have to lose?

Do not let a bad evangelism experience or the lack of evangelistic experience keep you from sharing in the greatest mission the world has ever known. You will never know how great it is until you try it.

Isn't it strange how one negative experience can adversely impact a lifetime?

I had a run in with a can of spinach at a critical point in my life. I was in that golden age when cartoons still captivated and kissing was gross. I spent a week with my grandparents during the summer and made some amazing memories.

Most of those memories had to do with food. I belong to a family that loves to eat.

I remember that each afternoon at 3:00 p.m. my grandmother would lay a blanket out in front of the television. She would then serve me a snack on that blanket while I watched cartoons. Every day she brought me something different like peanut butter crackers, Cheetos, Nilla Wafers, Little Debbie snack cakes, or saltines with Easy Cheese. There was always a frosty mug of root beer to wash it down.

For breakfast we had donuts and coffee. I was far too young

for coffee, but when I watched my grandfather dunk his donut, I had to try it to. That got me started on a lifelong coffee obsession.

Dinner was a special time as the three of us gathered around their small kitchen table for a hot meal. There was always some sort of meat, a starch, a vegetable, and dessert. Of course dessert could only be eaten if you cleaned your plate.

Cleaning my plate was never much of a problem. I loved my grandmother's cooking, and dessert was sufficient motivation. One night, though, I just could not do it.

I blame Popeye for the situation that unfolded. Earlier that day, as I watched cartoons, I declared to my grandparents that I wanted to be just like Popeye. Popeye was an ordinary guy, but when he ate spinach, he became super strong. He carried a can of spinach in his pocket for emergency situations. Whenever his archenemy, Brutus, got the upper hand, all Popeye had to do was open up a can.

I begged my grandmother to fix me some spinach. That turned out to be a huge mistake.

She found a can of spinach that she had stashed in the back of the pantry. I was not prepared for the dark green, slimy, foul-smelling glob of disgustingness that came out of that can. She heated it up on the stove and served it with dinner.

When she scooped it onto my plate, I instantly realized that there would be no dessert for me. There was no way that stuff was going to go into my mouth. I no longer wanted to be like Popeye. The cost was just too high.

After a great deal of coercion, guilt, and a few threats, they convinced me to try one bite. It was awful. It tasted worse than it looked and smelled. I was wounded for life.

I made a decision that day that I did not like spinach. In fact, I decided that I did not like green vegetables of any kind. For years I refused to eat them. I was outspoken against them. I ridiculed vegetable eaters and would not listen to reason.

Finally someone put my manhood to the test by daring me to eat some spinach. They told me that it was fresh spinach and that it was different from the slimy canned stuff I had tried as a kid. I put a small piece in my mouth and found that I did not gag. I tried another piece and discovered that I did indeed like it.

It turns out that I enjoy all kinds of green vegetables. I love broccoli, brussels sprouts, peas, green beans, and asparagus (even though it makes my pee smell funny). I can't believe that I missed out on something so wonderful for so long just because I wouldn't try it.

Now what about you?

Will you pray for One? Will you try it?

I dare you. I triple dog dare you.

PLANT

The basic principles of farming are pretty easy to understand.

Decide what you want to grow and then plant the appropriate seed.

That's basically it.

You can adjust the variables some by adding water, picking locations based on sunlight or soil types, and guarding against pests. But you really cannot get inside the soil and make the seed grow. All you can do is decide what you want to grow and then plant the appropriate seed.

This is what your life comes down to. What do you want to grow?

> *"Do not be deceived: God cannot be mocked. A man reaps what he sows. Whoever sows to please their flesh, from the flesh will reap destruction; whoever sows to please the Spirit, from the Spirit will reap eternal life. Let us not become weary in doing good, for at the proper time we will reap a harvest if we do not give up."*
>
> **Galatians 6:7-9**

So many people are thoroughly deceived. They believe that they can grow something that they never planted. **They stare at the ground in confusion and wonder why God's promises are not being fulfilled in their lives, when in reality, they planted the wrong seeds.**

Do not be deceived. Do not fall for the lie that says the crop will just magically appear. It does not work that way. Faith is only good if it is accompanied by action. God gives you seeds, but if you do nothing with them, don't expect a crop. Disappointment rules the day for many Christians because they know enough to know that this world will never satisfy, but they don't trust enough to plant for the world to come.

God cannot be mocked. Everything will be revealed for what it is. Every church that refused to plant will give an account. Every Christian who squandered his or her life will have to answer to Jesus. Do not mock God by pretending that it does not matter. God is not amused by our foolishness. The stakes are high, and He has entrusted us with the seed of His gospel. Refusing to plant is the worst kind of mockery.

We reap what we sow. This is a simple logic statement. It is not a threat from some kind of cosmic, killjoy in the sky waiting to rain down lightning bolts on everyone who disobeys. If you spend your life planting seeds for the here and now, when the here and now is destroyed, everything you planted will be destroyed as well. The here and now will be destroyed. It will not last. This world is fading fast. One of two things will happen in your lifetime. Either Jesus will return, or you will die. Either way, the end is near! What will you have to show at the end? You reap what you sow. If you are not planting for eternity, then you will reap nothing in eternity.

Do not weary in doing good. A harvest is coming. Plant for the harvest God desires. Scatter seeds of faith. Pray for One and share God's love with others.

Only a total fool would plant pumpkin seeds and expect sunflowers to grow. But many Christians will come to the end of their lives and wonder how they managed to plant nothing of eternal value. Do not be a fool. God entrusts you with His gospel. Plant. Then plant again. Then plant some more. Plant until you can plant no more because you have left this life for the life to come.

THINK ABOUT IT

1. What do you want your life to produce? Seriously think about this and answer honestly. What matters most to you?

2. What are you planting? Does what you are planting line up with what you want to produce?

3. Are you planting what God wants you to plant? Is your life more focused on producing an eternal harvest or an earthly harvest?

4. How can you be more proactive in planting the gospel in the hearts of your Ones?

PRAY ABOUT IT

Seeks God's best. Drop any defensiveness and justification. Ask God to give you a vision of what you are planting. Pray that your will would be aligned to His so that He will use you to help more people into the Kingdom of Heaven.

NOTES:

ACCOUNT

Pay attention.

This is important.

You are going to die.

Seriously. You are not long for this world. The end is near. Death is on your doorstep. You can pretend, fight, and ignore all you want, but it does not change reality.

> *"This is why it is said: 'Wake up, sleeper, rise from the dead, and Christ will shine on you.'*
> *Be very careful, then, how you live—not as unwise but as wise, making the most of every opportunity, because the days are evil. Therefore do not be foolish, but understand what the Lord's will is."*
>
> **Ephesians 5:14-17**

Wake up. Do not waste the life you have left. Do not be a fool. Understand the Lord's will.

The Lord's will is not difficult to ascertain. Jesus was clear regarding His will.

> *"What do you think? If a man owns a hundred sheep, and one of them wanders away, will he not leave the ninety-nine on the hills and go to look for the one that wandered off? And if he finds it, truly I tell you, he is happier about that one sheep than about the ninety-nine that did not wander off. In the same way your Father in heaven is not willing that any of these little ones should perish."*
>
> **Matthew 18:12-14**

God's will is that none would perish. God wants every lost One to be found. If you are His servant, then you must live to do His will. Living for less is not living at all. Any other purpose is merely a march toward death. Too many people are living to die instead of dying to live. When we die to self and our selfish desires, we are free to finally live eternally. We escape the confines of time, space, and mortality when our hearts align with God's and His will is accomplished through us.

A day of judgment is coming. Christ will return and each person will give an account for how they used the life that was entrusted to them. Christ's presence will burn away every impurity. Nothing temporary will be left. Only the eternal things of God will remain. **What will you have to show for your years on earth? Will your account be empty or full?**

Pray for One and grab hold of what matters most.

> *"Be merciful to those who doubt; save others by snatching them from the fire."*
> **Jude 1:22-23**

Who is your One? Who is God compelling you to go share His love with? What are you waiting for? Go now. Lead a life of no regrets. No one will ever bow before Jesus and regret all the Ones they snatched from the fire, but many will bow before Jesus and mourn the Ones they let slip away.

THINK ABOUT IT

1. If Jesus came back right now, what eternal value would your life have? If all the temporary things of life immediately were burned away, what would you have left?

2. Do you have any regrets for how you have lived? What are they? How can you move beyond regrets into a life that matters?

3. Who are your Ones? What are their names? What would happen to them if Jesus came back today?

PRAY ABOUT IT

Prayerfully picture yourself before Jesus at Judgment Day. Ask Him what He will say to you? Ask Him to give you a vision of a life well lived in Him. Pray for One and ask God to save your Ones.

NOTES:

DAY 40

CHICKEN

By the time this goes to print, it will probably be politically incorrect to call someone who is controlled by fear "chicken." I understand the risk I am taking with the poultry aficionados. Those who defend the chicken as a noble bird with courageous character should probably stop reading now because I am about to ruffle some feathers.

So here we go. Chickens do not pray for One.

Chickens only care about self-preservation.

Listen to how Christians often talk to one another. What are their primary concerns? Far too much time, attention, and energy is wasted on fearful exercises of the me-centered theology they cling to.

They are afraid politically because our country is going to Hell in a hand basket as our "Christian" nation is destroyed. They are afraid economically because everyone knows that good Christians prosper financially and bad Christians struggle. They are afraid physically because declining health is a stark reminder that their hope is squarely planted in the here and now and not in the life to come. They are afraid relationally because the thought of being taken advantage of is more than they can bear so they have shut themselves off and do not allow God's love to flow through them.

Chickens.

Then you have the religious leaders who profit from the fear. They control and manipulate their churches. They feed the chickens and keep them cooped up in their little hen houses.

They rule the roost and lay a big fat egg. Nothing is done to build God's Kingdom. Nobody is saved. Fear is the only thing perpetuated.

Chickens.

Chickens will write off praying for One as being too evangelistically focused. What? Think about the absurdity of that. How can anything be too focused on Christ's mission? That is an asinine notion.

Chickens will not pray for One because of the potential cost. Pastors might fear losing their jobs. Leaders might fear losing their power and influence. Members might fear losing their favorite church programs. Everyone probably fears the financial cost. Praying for One is never cheap.

Chickens will not pray for One because chickens fear change. Change is coming if you pray for One. Imagine an entire church praying for One. What would a church look like if every member was passionately focused on storming the gates of Hell to set the captives free?

Chickens.

"Have I not commanded you? Be strong and courageous. Do not be afraid; do not be discouraged, for the LORD your God will be with you wherever you go."
Joshua 1:9

Do not be a chicken. Pray for One. I dare you.

Why did the Christian cross the road? To find the chicken on the other side.

THINK ABOUT IT

1. What fears do you have about praying for One?

2. What does God think about your fears?

3. What obstacles might prevent you from asking God to give you One to share His love with?

4. What does God value most? What do you value most? What does your church value most?

PRAY ABOUT IT

Ask God to reveal any fears within you that prevent you from doing His will. Confess your fears to Him and ask for His courage. Pray for strength to endure any trouble that may come from praying for One.

NOTES:

FROM BILL

chapter twelve

FROM BILL

I have received hundreds of Praying for One stories. All of them are impactful, powerful, and inspiring. I would love to include them all in this book, but time and space do not allow for such indulgences.

I have returned to one story over and over again throughout the writing of this book. The story is simple, short, and thoroughly profound. This story captures the essence of praying for One, and I leave it for you to ponder in your heart.

The following was taken from an email that was sent to me by a man named Bill.

A neighbor found her down by the river, no shoes or socks, her feet dirty and bleeding.

She was crying and hysterical.

He brought her to us, because he knew we would help her.

We hugged her and told her we loved her. We knelt down, took a warm washcloth from the kitchen, and washed her feet. We found a pair of socks and shoes her size and put them on her feet. We fed, hugged, and prayed with her.

She accepted Christ that morning, and we were joyous.

Three days later she died of a drug overdose, and we were devastated.

We were consoled that God knew she would die that week. He wanted her to accept His son before she died, so He brought her to us.

We prayed for One, God sent One to us, and now she is with Him for eternity.

We continue to pray for One.

- Bill

Then Jesus told them this parable: "Suppose one of you has a hundred sheep and loses one of them. Doesn't he leave the ninety-nine in the open country and go after the lost sheep until he finds it? And when he finds it, he joyfully puts it on his shoulders and goes home. Then he calls his friends and neighbors together and says, 'Rejoice with me; I have found my lost sheep.' I tell you that in the same way there will be more rejoicing in heaven over one sinner who repents than over ninety-nine righteous persons who do not need to repent.

Luke 15:3-7

STORY

When you pray for One, you become part of God's story.

Hopefully you have prayed for One and are aware of God's answers to your prayers. Have you experienced a pray for One moment? How did it go? Did you respond? Did you miss it? What happened?

> *"As for us, we cannot help speaking about what we have seen and heard."*
>
> **Acts 4:20**

Use day forty-one to tell your story. Then keep telling your story from this day on.

NOTES:

About the Author

Bo Chancey is the senior pastor of Manchester Christian Church in Manchester, New Hampshire. Bo is a gifted communicator who is passionate about challenging people to fall madly in love with Jesus Christ. He believes that church should be fun and that God desperately desires all people to find the freedom of living an abundant life in Him.

Bo received a degree in History and Speech Communications at Texas A&M University. He and his wife, Somer have three children: Alizah, Aysen and Ensley. Bo enjoys sports, writing songs, spending time with his family and preaching.

facebook.com/bochancey

twitter.com/bochancey

Other Books by Bo

I'm Going to Light Myself on Fire

Every Day with Jesus

What's Your Problem

Another Day with Jesus

Find these and other titles at amazon.com.